*Human Suffering and the
Evil of Religion*

Human Suffering and the Evil of Religion

The Greatest Problems for Belief in God

Dennis Jensen

RESOURCE *Publications* · Eugene, Oregon

HUMAN SUFFERING AND THE EVIL OF RELIGION
The Greatest Problems for Belief in God

Copyright © 2018 Dennis Jensen. All rights reserved. Except for brief quotations in critical publications or reviews, no part of this book may be reproduced in any manner without prior written permission from the publisher. Write: Permissions, Wipf and Stock Publishers, 199 W. 8th Ave., Suite 3, Eugene, OR 97401.

Resource Publications
An Imprint of Wipf and Stock Publishers
199 W. 8th Ave., Suite 3
Eugene, OR 97401

www.wipfandstock.com

PAPERBACK ISBN: 978-1-5326-4343-9
HARDCOVER ISBN: 978-1-5326-4344-6
EBOOK ISBN: 978-1-5326-4345-3

Manufactured in the U.S.A.

All scripture quotations, unless otherwise indicated, are taken from the Holy Bible, New International Version®, NIV®. Copyright ©1973, 1978, 1984, 2011 by Biblica, Inc.™ Used by permission of Zondervan. All rights reserved worldwide. www.zondervan.com The "NIV" and "New International Version" are trademarks registered in the United States Patent and Trademark Office by Biblica, Inc.™

Scripture quotations marked (LEB) are from the *Lexham English Bible*. Copyright © 2012 Logos Bible Software. Lexham is a registered trademark of Logos Bible Software. Used by permission. All rights reserved.

Scripture quotations marked (NASB) are taken from the NEW AMERICAN STANDARD BIBLE ®, Copyright © 1960, 1962, 1963, 1968, 1971, 1972, 1973, 1975, 1977, 1995 by The Lockman Foundation. Used by permission.

Scripture quotations marked (NKJV) are taken from the New King James Version®. Copyright © 1982 by Thomas Nelson. Used by permission. All rights reserved.

Scripture quotations marked (RSV) are from the Revised Standard Version of the Bible, copyright © 1946, 1952, and 1971 the Division of Christian Education of the National Council of the Churches of Christ in the United States of America. Used by permission. All rights reserved.

Portions of a talk given by Lee Strobel at Cherry Hills Community Church, Highlands Ranch, CO, March 12, 2011 are printed by permission.

Contents

Acknowledgments | ix
Introduction | xi

Part I: Human Suffering, The Greatest Problem for Belief in God

1. Plantinga's Insight | 3
2. The Recipient Oriented Free Will Theodicy | 10
3. Other Biblical Answers | 20
4. Biblical Support for the Recipient Oriented Theodicy | 26
5. Foreknowledge and the Testing Theodicies | 30
6. The Problem of Lost Loved Ones | 34
7. The Observer Oriented Free Will Theodicy | 39
8. Salvation for the Unborn | 43
9. The Insufficiency of the Agent and Observer Oriented Theodicies | 49
10. Summary | 52

Part II: Bad Religion?

11. What Makes a Religion Bad? | 59
12. Are the Religious Worse than the Secular? | 63
13. What Good Comes from Christianity? | 71
14. Biblical Discrimination and Oppression | 89
15. Does Religion Promote Superstition? | 102

Contents

16. Hard Hearts and Bad Laws | 105
17. Women and the Bible | 108
18. Slavery | 117
19. Is the New Testament Anti-Semitic? | 121
20. The Canaanite Conquest | 126
21. Can Child Molesters Go to Heaven? | 132
22. Atheism's Moral Problem | 135
23. Summary | 143

Bibliography | 149

Acknowledgments

My special thanks to Lisa Guinther who proofread my text and offered invaluable suggestions. Though I was unable to incorporate all of the suggestions Lisa offered, those I included made this book much better and definitely more readable than it would have been without her help.

Introduction

THIS IS A BOOK about possible answers to some of our hardest questions concerning belief in God. Foremost in many people's thinking would be, Why has God allowed the suffering, sometime very extreme suffering, we find in the world? If we have in the Bible a message from God then shouldn't we hope to find there answers to this question?

I believe the reader will discover some very feasible and persuasive answers. We will first look at the basic notion that we should not expect to know what an all knowing God's reason for allowing any given suffering might be. Then we will consider the idea suggested in the book of Job that God wishes to know (maybe even needs to know) how we will respond to God for allowing us this suffering. Do we just serve or love God because of the good he does for us (Job 1:9–10)? Finally we will look at the claim found so often in the Bible that God allows some suffering to see whether we will choose to seek to have God's heart. Will we hurt for those who are hurting; will we anguish over them as God does? Will we seek to alleviate their suffering? By these different choices we become something we never could become without them. In examining these questions we will also need to look at the most important difficulties which accompany these claims.

The second part of this book will look at a question related to the general problem of suffering, Does religion cause more harm to the world than good? And even more specifically, Does Christianity produce more harm than good? If both do produce such harm, would this not give us reason to think religions in general, and especially Christianity, should be rejected? To be honest, this would not give us reason to think that any religion is false but it might bring us to avoid seriously embracing or even looking into such a religion. The first part of the book asks how religion answers the problem of human suffering, the second part asks if religion produces suffering.

Introduction

I will argue that some religions might certainly be the source of much suffering or evil but this depends on several factors, factors such as the ethical content of those religions. I will also argue that Christianity does not produce more evil than good. That is, if one seeks to follow the original teachings of Jesus and his first followers, it produces more overall good than harm.

Perhaps more interesting will be our attempt to see how the great evils of which Christianity is often accused—the Inquisition, the pograms, the witch hunts—how these horrible cancers to the world's well-being came to be if Christianity is at its core good. Might we expect the same kind of horrors if Christianity had never been?

A related issue we will look at is the problem of the evils that result from God's purported commands and actions in the Bible. Did God command the Israelites to slaughter innocent children? Did God himself wipe out most of the human race by a flood? Was it right to have people executed for merely picking up sticks on the Sabbath? Does the Bible condemn homosexual behavior or denigrate women? Should such acts and commands be thought of as evil and should the biblical God be judged to be evil? The answers to these questions will have much to do with how Christianity must be judged since it says that this God is absolutely good and deserves our highest honor, praise, and love.

I have tried to keep my arguments on a non-academic level. My main concern has been to look at certain problems with belief in God and Christianity. I have not looked at any of the positive evidence for belief. Since I will not deal with this issue again, the following footnote will provide a short list of works for anyone interested in the positive evidence.[1]

---

1. I believe the best initial evidence for belief in God and for Christianity would be the following:

1) William Lane Craig, *On Guard for Students*.

2) Probably the most important or core evidence for Christianity is the evidence for the resurrection of Jesus. To begin to look into this in more detail, see Habermas and Licona, *The Case for the Resurrection of Jesus*.

3) The evidence from messianic prophecy is a second common source of evidence for Christianity. For this, see first Rydelnik, *The Messianic Hope*.

4) One important prophecy Rydelnik mentions but does not fully deal with is found in Daniel 9. Harold Hoehner argues that given some fairly reasonable assumptions, this prophecy is fulfilled to the day by Jesus' triumphal entry into Jerusalem a week before his death. (Omitting the weaker of these assumptions, it can be argued to be fulfilled within a month of the time prophesied.) So the prophecy indicates fairly precisely when Messiah will appear on earth. Hoehner's argument is found in *Chronological Aspects of the Life of Christ*, chap. 6. I have evaluated a similar argument based primarily on Hoehner's

Introduction

The two parts of this book can fairly easily be read independently of each other. However, I hope the reader will find that the arguments in the two compliment each other, that information from one study will provide insights into the second.

The reader will notice that I have often referenced statements with scriptural passages and provided arguments that a particular belief is a biblical view by looking closely at passages in the Bible. I hope readers will not find this to appear sermonic. My intention is to give a good case that these are clearly biblical views and to see if these views answer certain critiques of Christianity.

---

evidence but with some additional information. This may be found at Jensen, "The Time of Messiah."

Part I

Human Suffering, The Greatest Problem for Belief in God

1

Plantinga's Insight

PROBABLY THE MOST IMPORTANT objection to belief in God historically, on both a scholarly and a popular level, is the Problem of Evil. If there is an all good, powerful, and intelligent God, why is there so much suffering in the world? Many believe that there is so much evil that this would not be expected from a good creator.

Perhaps the best answer to this expectation can be arrived at through merely thinking through the logic of the claim. With Alvin Plantinga's work in the mid-1970s and earlier, I think that the basic Problem of Evil as a rational philosophical problem has essentially been answered.[1] I would want to focus on one of his more important arguments. If there is a God who is all knowing and all good, and since our knowledge is very limited, we should not expect to know what such a God's reason may be for allowing evil to allow a greater good to occur. There is no good reason to say that such a God would have no such reason. This type of approach is called skeptical theism. If this God is omniscient, all knowing, my knowledge compared to God's would be closer to that of my cat's knowledge to my own. (Similar analogies will appear in the course of our discussions.) Clearly one would not have good reason to think God does not have good reason for allowing the evils which occur.

Plantinga was not the first to see this, of course. Indeed, it is often pointed out that this is the response or defense we find near the close of the book of Job in the Bible (Job 38–41). Here God speaks to Job but does

---

1. Plantinga, *Nature of Necessity*, chap. 9; *God, Freedom, and Evil*, 7–29, esp. 10; *God and Other Minds*, 107–30.

not tell him why he is given so much undeserved suffering. Yet God does demonstrate to Job that he should expect that God does have good reason for allowing it.

Many people look at God's speech at the end of Job as a tyrant's demand for complete obedience no matter what his reason for allowing this suffering. They hear him say, "I'm God, how dare you question my actions!" But God is here constantly referring to his wisdom, pointing out that Job did not and does not experience or know all that God knows or experiences. So the more likely understanding of God's speech is simply that we should not expect to know God's reasons for allowing suffering but we should expect that God does have morally justifying reason.

Suppose we attempt to assess two events G and E which have moral content. With our limited understanding we see that G only produces much good while E only produces much evil. If we had a choice as to which should occur, we should seek for G to occur and not E. We should act according to the limited knowledge we possess. But if God decides E should occur rather than G, this should not be considered questionable since God would know that a full outcome of good would be produced by E which would be greater than any evil it produces and any good G produces.

As an analogy we might think of the child who must undergo a painful medical procedure fully awake and without anesthesia. This is sometimes necessary to correct an injury or disease which would otherwise produce far greater suffering. Let's assume that the child is not old enough intellectually or emotionally to understand its necessity. Imagine the parents holding the child down as the physician works and the child looking into their eyes in unbelief. The parents can say nothing to bring the child to understand. You know what is going through her mind: "You of all people say you love me and yet you let this man do this to me?!" If our intelligence compared to God's is like the child's to her parents', might we think the same when in fact God has good reason for allowing pain? The child can only see that G, being free of the painful surgery, only produces good while E, enduring the scalpel, only produces evil. She is not aware of the greater good that will come if E occurs.

As a biblical example, Caiaphas, the high priest at the time of Jesus' death, made the first legal decision to condemn Jesus. This ostensively produced more evil than good and, if Caiaphas had knowledge of Jesus' claims as the Gospels say, he will not be guiltless for his decision. Nevertheless, if the Christian view is correct that Jesus' death provided salvation for humanity, then in the long run Caiaphas's decision produced more good than had he not condemned Jesus.

Another example, this time from the Hebrew scripture, would be the story of Joseph (Gen 37, 39–47). Joseph and his bothers were the sons of Jacob and the great grandsons of Abraham. Joseph's brothers hated him because of the special favor their father showed him and because he had dreams suggesting his brothers would submit to him. Without his father's knowledge, they sold him into slavery and let Jacob think he was killed by a wild animal.

In Egypt Joseph was eventually imprisoned but, as the story goes, through a connection with Pharaoh he later was able to give the interpretation of a dream which saved the country from famine. He was given a high position in the government and was able to have his family come to Egypt and escape the famine. Joseph later told his brothers who sold him into slavery that they intended their actions for evil, but God intended them for good (Gen 50:20). With these examples it is not difficult to imagine that some great evil might be needed to produce a greater good.

The brothers were still guilty of selling Joseph into slavery. Only if they had had the full knowledge God had of his plan to save Israel through this act would they have been innocent of selling Joseph into slavery. We are responsible to do good only given our limited awareness of the final good or evil which results. If G appears to us to produce more good and less evil than E, our moral obligation is to do G and not to do E. This is so even if it turns out that God intends E to occur in order to produce a greater good.

Charitable organizations are aware that attempts to help impoverished areas of the world sometimes result in new socially harmful conditions. There are cases in which they have introduced new technologies (drought resistant crops, better wells, etc.) thus increasing the people's standard of living. Sometimes these changes have resulted in new problems such as increased alcoholism, gambling, prostitution, drug abuse, new diseases, etc. This certainly should not stop these organizations and those who support them from continuing to help these depressed areas to develop economically even if they cannot find ways to alleviate the new problems.

But God may see the final amount of good or evil which would result and determine that the greater good would be that the changes the charity would like to implement should not occur. So God might hinder or stop them from doing a particular work. Yet without having God's full knowledge, we should always seek to support such economic development in depressed parts of the world. We should do so even if we can foresee that some of the new problems will likely result.

It might appear that skeptical theism would say that whenever any evil occurs, no matter how bad it is, it must be better than had it not occurred at all. Would it not follow that the skeptical theist should not oppose or seek to remove any evil they know of? No. God may have a reason for allowing a certain evil but that reason may be contingent upon the choices and actions of others. I will suggest some such reasons later. So God may allow some evils and also want to either remove them or reduce their force. We should seek to remove almost any suffering or oppression we know of. Only if we are absolutely sure that God is allowing some suffering which God wants to remain undiminished should we refrain from seeking to end it or diminish its force.

Before going much further, I would like to offer some basic terms in order to understand the kinds of approaches one may take to look at the problem of suffering generally. A *theistic defense* is an argument that God has reasons for allowing evil but it is also an argument which may be given with or without offering such possible reasons. One need not give or even have any idea what those reasons might be. Plantinga's skeptical theistic approach is thus a theistic defense. In contrast to a theistic defense, a *theodicy* is an answer to the Problem of Evil given by seeking to explain God's actual reason or reasons for allowing evil. So the last two biblical examples we have just looked at are, strictly speaking, theodicies for specific evils. We will look at some more theodicies shortly. Some theistic defenses, like a free will defense, will offer possible reasons God allows evil without claiming these reasons are necessarily the actual reasons God has for doing so. If it is merely a possible and reasonable explanation, this should be sufficient to show that the Problem of Evil has no force. Theodicies, on the other hand, claim that this "real possibility is God's *actual* justification for permitting evil."[2]

Once skeptical theism is understood, it should be clear that the critic also has no good reason to claim that God *probably* does not have good reason for allowing the amount and kind of horrendous evil that is present in our world.[3] Isn't it at least more likely, they may say, that God does not have good reason for letting an innocent child suffer a long, agonizing,

---

2. Goetz, "Argument from Evil," 454.

3. Since Plantinga's work, critics have tended to shift to this approach. See Howard-Snyder, *Evidential Argument from Evil* for such arguments as well as notable skeptical theistic responses (e.g., Alston's articles for the latter).

Plantinga's Insight

gruesome death by hanging in a Nazi concentration camp? Well, no it isn't. Probability just does not apply if we cannot know God's mind since God's intelligence is enormously greater than ours.

God may not be able to share his reasons for human pain and suffering because the human mind would not be able to comprehend the explanations. When we look at the specific theodicies we will consider shortly, it will become acutely obvious that simply because we are not now able to think of a reason God may have allowed a certain kind of suffering does not give us reason to think that there likely is no such reason.

It is not difficult to imagine certain conditions under which a creator of the universe could be rightly judged to be evil. Suppose, for example, we imagine God effecting very great, unending, undiminishing torment of someone who does not deserve it. (Of course, if by definition God must be absolutely good, as must be the case if this God is deserving of our worship, God could not do such a thing.) But notice first of all that no such suffering can occur in any person's lifetime. Not only must all suffering end with death, even with the most painful earthly suffering imaginable, it appears likely that the human body engages a natural self-anesthetization system utilizing endorphins, serotonin, or possibly other pain inhibitors. Nevertheless, even if very great but temporary undeserved suffering is allowed, on the possibility that it is recompensed and that God has good reason for allowing it, God cannot be judged to be evil. With one qualification I will note below, we cannot say that any given suffering in this life, no matter how horrible it may be, cannot result in a greater good if caused or allowed by an all powerful and knowing being.

Some suffering may be gratuitous in the sense of producing in itself no overriding good. A good God could have a wider reason for giving us an environment of suffering that will be compensated overall yet without each particular point of suffering producing in itself a greater good. Such gratuitous evils would normally be relatively few or insignificant. God would more often want to use instances of suffering to produce in themselves greater good.[4]

I would also want to claim that it is a mistake for skeptical theists to suggest that the reason for seemingly gratuitous evils will always be found in the occurrence of some good outcome in a time or location in this world. Though it is certainly true that some evils can be explained in this way, they need to emphasize that many evils may only fully result in an overriding good in our lives in a world other than this one.

4. Cf. MacGregor, "Gratuitous Evil," 165–80.

Part I: Human Suffering, The Greatest Problem for Belief in God

Child Suffering

In his debate with William Lane Craig, Sam Harris presented one of his complaints against belief in God by looking at the problem of the death and suffering of children. Though Harris's particular arguments had little to do with the topic of the debate, we will find his claims to be useful for our purposes as we look at the basic Problem of Evil. I will use child suffering as a primary example to look at this problem in general.

He says that twenty-four thousand children under five die each day and asks us to "think of the parents of these children."

> Most of these men and women believe in God and are praying at this moment for their children to be spared. And their prayers will not be answered.... But... this is all a part of God's plan. Any God who would allow children by the millions to suffer and die in this way, and their parents to grieve in this way, either can do nothing to help them, or doesn't care to. He is either impotent or evil. ...
> ... When children by the tens of thousands are torn from their parents' arms and drowned [as so many were with the 2004 tsunami], we're told that God is mysterious.[5]

Harris attempts to make Plantinga's insight into a caricature. When he says that Christians just respond to some enormous evil with, "Ah, but God's ways are mysterious," he is suggesting that this is being evasive since it's most obvious that God is caught in an embarrassing situation and Christians are trying to avoid having anyone notice the problem. We see here a tacit assumption in Harris's accusation and in the evidential argument from evil. It is assumed that we know enough about "everything there is to know" to establish some probability that God has no good reason for allowing some evils. But the possibility that there is still far too much unknown to us, possibly far more than we could ever imagine, essentially undercuts this belief.

To more fully answer the Problem of Evil in a way that is more humanly or emotionally satisfying, we need more than skeptical theism's purely logical answer. But if we are looking at the problem on a completely rational level, that answer is all we need. God's ways and knowledge are, indeed, "mysterious," and beyond our knowledge by the attributes we would assume God possesses. We should *not* expect to know what God's reason

---

5. Craig vs. Harris; Harris, first rebuttal, par. 2, 5.

is for allowing the evil we experience nor do we have any reason to suspect that there is no such reason.

Though I think we should admit that we should not expect to know or understand what God's reasons are for allowing evil, we should recognize that the Bible does give us at least some purported reasons. I would want to claim that much of the Christian's defense of their beliefs is much weaker than it could be simply because it does not often present the more biblical responses or theodicies.

We need to look at two final issues before considering some of these possible answers to the problem of suffering. These possible answers may involve claims like the assertion that all who suffer will experience a complete compensating good for their pain or that there exists a heaven in which some (or maybe even everyone) will experience eternal bliss. At least these are the kinds of claims which might be made. Anyone who attempts to defend a belief in a good creator God does not need to give good reasons to believe that, say, such a heaven exists. One only needs to offer a possible state of affairs.

The basic accusation from the Problem of Evil is that a good God cannot exist since certain evils exist. It is claimed that there is some kind of contradiction or inconsistency between these two propositions. The burden of proof is on the shoulders of the person making this accusation. Anyone who seeks to respond to or defeat this accusation need only present the possibility of the existence of this heaven (and whatever other claimed state of affairs would adequately do the job). Since the proposition the critic wishes to refute assumes the existence of a God who allows undeserved suffering, it is no less likely that such a God could create such a heaven.

The difficult issue would be determining exactly what one would need that would adequately answer the problem. That is the question we will look at in the next section. For example, we should ask questions like, Would the existence of a heaven for those who have suffered undeserved pain solve the problem? What would be an adequate reason for the suffering? etc. One does not need to give evidence that such a heaven exists.

The second issue we will need to consider is whether or how well any such proposed answers accord with biblical teaching. Is there a clearly Christian answer to the Problem of Evil? Much of this study will thus be concerned to discuss not only how reasonable a given proposal is to answer the problem, but also how biblical it is.

2

The Recipient Oriented Free Will Theodicy

SOME SUFFERING IS DESERVED. With enough conditions or caveats we might imagine that a child's death could sometimes be a punishment for an adult. As a biblical example, look at 2 Samuel 12:14. For the sins of murder and adultery David repented and God forgave him and yet God still required that he be punished. One of his punishments was that his recently born son would die. The death of a child to punish a parent might give us a partial answer as to why some children die but it would not resolve the problem for the child. So this is hardly a sufficient response even for those cases in which the parent does deserve punishment. The more difficult issue is the *undeserved* suffering of the child. Much of the scripture, like the first two chapters of the book of Job, assumes that much of our suffering is undeserved.

Before we talk about undeserved suffering for the child, we need to consider what I would argue to be one of the most basic reasons the Bible offers for undeserved suffering for a responsible moral agent such as a bereaved parent. This is the Patient or Recipient Oriented Free Will Theodicy. It asks the recipient of undeserved suffering how they will respond to God in the face of that suffering. The most important choice we will make in this life involves how we will respond to God when God allows us to suffer. For this testing to take place we have to endure some pain though the amount may vary with the individual. There may also be other factors which determine the amount of suffering one must endure which we will talk about later. This theodicy also says that all undeserved suffering will

The Recipient Oriented Free Will Theodicy

be recompensed, that those who endure undeserved suffering will be given some kind of compensating good.

To help establish the importance of this particular approach, we will also look at other reasons given in the Bible for human suffering. We will attempt to see how the Recipient Oriented Theodicy relates to these other answers.

God sometimes asks, "Are you willing to give up everything you've wanted most, if I ask you to?" That's what God asked Abraham when he asked him to sacrifice his son. That's what God asked of Job when he took away his possessions, his children, and his friends, and then allowed him to be stricken with a terrible, painful disease. Sometimes we will respond, "God, if that's what you are really like, then no, I won't. You don't deserve my commitment, my trust, not if you ask something like this of me."

If we were to imagine God answering back we might hear God say, "Why do you say, 'If that's what I'm really like'? Do you think it is wrong of me to ask this of you? I'm taking from you the child you love, the child you love more than anything else. You will have her back again, but just not now. But because you have to wait, because you aren't willing to wait, do you reject me for doing this?

"No, there is nothing I've done or can do for which you can say that I am evil. I still deserve your commitment and love. And I know that what I ask of you isn't easy. Indeed, that is why I ask it. I ask it because I have to know what your choice will be. Are you willing to endure this hardship, this loneliness, this missing the one you love so much, because I ask this of you? It's just a matter of waiting. Don't reject me just because you think it's too hard to wait. No, that's not a good reason.

"I'm your Creator, I'm your Source. I gave you life. I can be your closest friend, your joy, your nearest companion and confidant. That's what I was meant to be for you. I made you this way. I made you so that you could never be complete until you know and love me. I couldn't have made you any other way.

"I'm the one who deserves your deepest and greatest love and commitment. Don't reject me because, for just a little while, I choose to separate you from the child you love.

"To be tested, sometimes I will take something you want very much. Sometimes I will test you by allowing pain to come to you. I need to know what you will choose. If you do not pass the test, it is still better that you be tested than that you never know pain."

Part I: Human Suffering, The Greatest Problem for Belief in God

This theodicy or reason God allows evil applies to emotional and psychological pain such as the loss of a beloved child and it also applies to actual physical pain. It answers the most basic problem of moral evil as well as natural evil insofar as natural evil affects people. Natural evil is the suffering caused by impersonal forces of nature like earthquakes, disease, famine, flood, etc. Moral evil is suffering caused by the evil moral choices of humans or other conscious moral agents other than God (if there are any). This theodicy applies to Christians and other theists as well as atheists, those who seek God as well as those who have no concern about God. The atheist must ask, "If there is a God who deserves my commitment, would I admit my commitment to such a being even though this God has brought me great pain and suffering?"

All undeserved suffering will be recompensed, sometimes to the point that it will far outweigh the pain one has gone through. The apostle Paul said in essence that the suffering we now endure is not worth comparing to the joy, or "glory," we will have then (Rom 8:18; 2 Cor 4:17). Of course, Paul was specifically speaking about the compensation Christians receive. But if God is just, it also follows that this just compensation for undeserved suffering applies to all people, even those who reject God and are finally rejected by God.

Not only does God need to know if we will freely choose God in the face of suffering, we need to be people who make that choice. We become something new that we could not be without that choice. To freely make the choice of the good, I become good. To freely make the choice of evil, I become evil. God cannot make me good or evil in any sense of my being responsible for my acts; I have to freely choose. Notice that we need both. We need to become new creatures by our choices and God needs to know what our decisions will be.

It is vitally important that one becomes good by one's choices. Free will is outside of the control of God. God has the power to control the choices of all creatures but has willingly given up this power in order that a greater good would occur. Without creaturely free will God would simply make a person as good and great as they could possibly be short of that means. When they freely choose to do good, they become good in a way God cannot cause them to be, a way beyond the power of God.

Some readers may find the idea of something being beyond the power of God difficult to accept. But we need to understand that it is no limitation upon God's power, God's omnipotence, to admit that God cannot perform

The Recipient Oriented Free Will Theodicy

some actions so long as such actions are logically impossible. Just as it is logically impossible for God to make a square which is at the same time a circle, so it is impossible for God to make us as good as we could be by God's actions alone—to be good in that unique manner requires our free choice.

At this point because of the nature of this study I would not want to go any further to attempt to demonstrate this logical impossibility. I would rather want to claim only that intuitively we see that this is most likely true and that it cannot be demonstrated that it is not. We see that only our free choice to do good can make us good in a way God, without that choice, cannot.

We find this answer to the problem of undeserved suffering most ostensively in the book of Job, Job being the first book in the Bible to so strongly focus on this problem. Indeed, we may call this answer the most basic Jobian theodicy. Other answers to the problem of undeserved suffering are found in Hebrew and Christian scripture, but as we will see, this one is very basic to Hebrew thought and assumed throughout the Bible. I would claim that it is the most basic biblical theodicy for undeserved suffering.

Some have claimed that Job "has nothing to say to the puzzle of suffering." Indeed, this is the subtitle of a book by David Burrell. He dismisses this answer by diminishing the importance of the test but he provides no good reason for his claim. He also claims that no one can endure such a trial and completely ignores the many throughout history who clearly appear to have done so.[1]

Bart Ehrman puts the same basic criticism very graphically: "As satisfying as the book of Job has been to people over the ages, I have to say I find it supremely dissatisfying. If God tortures, maims, and murders people just to see how they will react—to see if they will not blame him, when in fact he is to blame—then this does not seem to me to be a God worthy of worship. Worthy of fear, yes. Of praise, no."[2]

This objection fails to fully understand the argument we find in the book of Job. We should have no problem admitting that God is responsible for this pain, if that is what Ehrman means by "blame," but we cannot say that God has done anything wrong. God allows this suffering (torture, maiming, etc.) to know how we will react, whether we will consider him guilty of doing wrong when in fact he is not. For God to allow this kind of

---

1. Burrell, *Deconstructing Theodicy*, 25.
2. Ehrman, *God's Problem*, 172.

suffering would not be evil since the far greater good that God has planned will come of it. Yes, the point is to see how people will respond to suffering with the degree of suffering never being more than what they are able to take, never being so great that they are forced to reject God. But the reason for the suffering is also to make them into something they could never become without this suffering. How they respond to God, both within and outside of the context of suffering, are the most crucial decisions they could ever make.

To freely turn to God or to turn against God makes us into people who are in the very core of our being either creatures who are, on our part, one with God or alienated from God. If God does eventually reconcile all people to himself and thus provide for them the greatest joy and fulfillment they could experience, still some will have marked themselves as those who would rather be alienated from God. Those who have chosen to be one with God have marked themselves, they have *created* themselves, to be those who have chosen what God has chosen; they have chosen to be wholly and completely God's children. God needs to see what that choice will be and we need to be creatures who so create ourselves.

With the recompense God provides, eventually the suffering will become as though it had never been. C. S. Lewis tells us that heaven works itself backwards.[3] Those in paradise will say, "I have never known pain." To some degree we can imagine this by thinking of experiencing the bliss of God's presence in paradise for infinite ages. Whether or not such an image can do justice to the claim, whether we can actually imagine how heaven works itself backward, we may not now know for certain. What we do know is that the Christian scripture does in fact promise that God will negate all such suffering. God will wipe away all of our tears.

Ehrman's error is that he thinks that allowing this suffering "just to see how they will react" to God is some trivial, childishly egotistical reason, whereas it is actually the very deepest reason for our existence. One wonders what he thinks the reason for our existence on earth might be. Does he think we are here to merely live a few score and ten years, to enjoy our families, raise children, maybe enjoy our labor and the company of friends? That's it? Anyone looking at life in this world objectively should see that these trivial explanations are not good reasons for our being here. These are not the kinds of reasons God would put us here. On the other hand, if God put us in a world which is so constructed as to allow us to freely choose for

---

3. Lewis, *The Great Divorce*, 69.

or against God at some time or another without excessive pressure either way, this would be the highest imaginable reason we could exist.

So if it is true that God does compensate for all undeserved suffering and that God has this extremely important reason for allowing this suffering, then God would still be good and bring it about that the greatest good will occur. Such a God would still deserve our highest worship and adoration.

Christian Narcissism?

Sam Harris has some other criticisms which may seem to apply at this point:

> This kind of faith . . . is really the perfection of narcissism. "God loves me, don'tcha know. He cured me of my eczema. He makes me feel so good while singing in church, . . . and just when we had given up hope, we found a banker who was willing to reduce my mother's mortgage."
>
> Ok, given all the good—all that this God of yours does not accomplish in the lives of others, . . . given the . . . misery that's being imposed on some helpless child at this instant, this kind of faith is obscene.[4]

We should be able to see how this criticism fails. We should be happy when good does happen to us. We should thank God for that. We should also hope for and pray for good to occur to all people and especially those who are greatly suffering. We should seek by any means we have to alleviate their suffering (a point we will discuss more later). The Christian who does not do this fails to fulfill their Lord's command. But we should also accept that if nothing we do can make a difference, though we should certainly continue to pray for them, this may be the trial that God has determined they must face. "The misery that's being imposed on some helpless child at this instant," as Harris puts it, may be necessary for the testing of the adult. Remember that the child will be given back full compensation for their suffering that will equal or far outweigh the suffering endured. In the long run the suffering will fulfill its purpose and only the good will be left.

Harris admits that he practices meditation himself, presumably to gain greater psychological peace, contentment, or stability. But the atheist who seeks inner peace is not more likely to be concerned about the plight of those who endure special hardship than the Christian who finds joy and

4. Craig vs. Harris; Harris, first rebuttal, par. 6, 7.

peace worshiping God. Indeed, Christians are motivated to be concerned about the needs of others in ways atheists cannot be. They desire a relationship with God; they want God's approval and dread God's disapproval. The basic Christian message, that of God's unfathomable love and sacrifice for us, motivates Christians to love and seek this God and to seek God's approval for their lives.

The Christian would have been more likely than the atheist to hide a Jewish person or family during the holocaust, for example. The atheist who believes this is their only life would be more likely to cling to their own life at all costs and refuse to hide such a family whereas the Christian would be motivated by God's promise of eternal reward and approval for carrying out such a morally courageous act. The Christian would be less apt to be concerned about the threat of death. In the second part of this book we will discuss more thoroughly whether religion, and specifically Christianity, are more beneficial than a world without religion or Christianity.

God's Megaphone

I should mention a popular Christian theodicy that may in fact involve or be a variation of the Recipient Oriented Theodicy. C. S. Lewis wrote a book entitled *The Problem of Pain*. One should probably look at that book in addition to or even before this one to better understand the context and reach of the problem as well as other serious answers to the problem. Lewis says, "God whispers to us in our pleasure, speaks to us in our conscience, but shouts to us in our pains: it is His megaphone to rouse a deaf world."[5] These are stimuli to turn back to God or to seek God for those who have no concern about God or who outright oppose God.

But why wouldn't God give us something else instead of pain, something which could be just as effective in drawing us to God? Why not a vision or religious experience? Wouldn't that better draw us to seek God or stimulate us to a deeper commitment to God? Well, something like that may come eventually, but usually God will use other normal human experiences to draw us to God before resorting to something like a religious experience. By allowing us pleasure, conscience, and pain God is able to search our minds and wills as well as to begin to stimulate us to seek God. They draw us to God by stimulating us, in different ways or degrees, to think about God as we would not have by other normal experiences. God honors the

5. Lewis, *Problem of Pain*, 93.

person who comes to seek God by these subtler and more natural means while letting them first come to their own decisions and conclusions. God honors them more than one who comes to God only by more overt and obvious supernatural means.

Pain brings me to contemplate and decide how I will respond to God. Of course, that may draw me to God or push me away. Everything hinges on my choice. But notice that the testing of my will is involved in this drawing to God. So the Recipient Oriented Theodicy is an important part of this drawing to God Lewis speaks about.

If I come to begin to seek God, I will eventually find God. At the end of the process I may need evidence as strong as a religious experience since God does not expect me to believe without sufficient evidence. Yet depending on the person, that religious experience need not be very strong. Something as weak as a sense of certainty that God is there or that Jesus is the promised Messiah may be all that God will give those for whom no more is needed. Or God may not even give a religious experience of any kind. God may simply lead one to new evidence or to see old evidence in a new light, evidence which the individual had once dismissed.

Lewis's theodicy may thus be seen as involving the Recipient Oriented Theodicy. God uses pain (as well as pleasure and conscience) to draw me to God but God also uses them to examine the depths of my heart and decisions.

I may completely rebel against God for allowing me such pain. The testing may, by my choice, bring me to reject God rather than to draw me to God. But in the process I choose to become something greater or something less than I was before and God sees and judges me by the choice I make. It is better to be able to make that choice than not. I must have this testing since this is the only way I could become something greater or better than I would be without it.

Do We Lose Compassion If Suffering Has a Reason?

Some popular atheists like Harris will tell us that if we can come up with good reasons God might allow some suffering then this would make us look at these poor souls with much less compassion. Think of those who have suffered greatly: the antebellum slave girl who is stripped, hung up by her wrists, and whipped to death; the Jewish baby in a concentration camp who is thrown alive onto a burning pile of wood. How can we weep for

Part I: Human Suffering, The Greatest Problem for Belief in God

them when we can think that within moments they will experience eternal bliss (or something like that) and that God had good reason for allowing this pain? How can we truly have compassion, how can our souls anguish over such unspeakable evils as indeed we should, unless we deny such answers and compensation? Whether we can come up with good reasons God may allow undeserved suffering, it is still better to disbelieve.

Harris does not understand that we can still accept that a greater good will come of one's suffering while still feeling anguish for that person. Think about Jesus' suffering. Imagine that the film, *The Passion of the Christ*, depicts something close to Jesus' actual pain. If Jesus himself fully comprehended what he would have to endure and yet he willingly chose to come to earth to do so, this makes the scourging, humiliation, abuse, and crucifixion even more agonizing.

Christians believe Jesus now and forever will have unimaginable joy and that he has provided by his death the greatest good humanity could ever experience, reconciliation with God. Even if this is true, none of this can erase for us the horror of what we see when we watch that film. It cannot erase the horror of what he went through. No matter how we might try to understand the good that came of his painful death, this does not make it any less shocking and repulsive and horrific.

That Jesus is not suffering now certainly does not make us feel indifferent to his suffering. It removes the utter despair some atheists experience when they witness or endure such suffering: the despair of believing that this suffering has no good to redeem it, that it will never do any good for anyone in any way, and that it will end in absolute annihilation, absolute nothingness. The Christian hope does remove that despair. But here we should ask ourselves, Is the atheist's despair—this bleakest of all despair, this despair which will never be alleviated so long as we are able to think about it—is this something we truly want to cling to if it could be removed? Is that what Harris really wants?

I find it amazing that the same people who complain about how horrible God must be to allow the pain we see in the world, how disgusting it is that God would do this, are often the same people who object if we find that God could have good reason for allowing it. They want to curse God for allowing this pain and they also want to curse God if God should have good reason for doing it, if God should redeem it and not allow the pain to end with its full force. They would rather have us wallow in unmitigated, hopeless despair.

The Recipient Oriented Free Will Theodicy

Think about what they are actually saying. By giving biblical answers as to why God allows suffering and by offering evidence that biblical Christianity is true, the Christian offers hope to those who suffer and to those who have loved ones who suffer horribly. For those whose suffering cannot be alleviated, the critic is saying that they just have to accept their pain. Think about some poor Jewish man who died in the holocaust after surviving for months under the deepest abuse and mistreatment and agony. The Harris-type atheist is telling him that this is just the way the world is and that he was just born at the wrong time and the wrong place. Perhaps the Harris-type atheist may feel compassion, maybe they can even agonize for the holocaust victim, but ultimately they have to tell him that there is nothing he can do about his situation so he has to just get used to it. As crass as this may seem, this is ultimately what they are saying. The Harris-atheist must ultimately lift his boot to grind his heel in the victim's face. He says, "No, don't offer hope, that will diminish their pain. It will make us less compassionate, less empathetic to their suffering." The claim put forward is that even if we can come up with good reasons for the suffering we see, it is still better to disbelieve. All in all, this claim fails.

3

Other Biblical Answers

AT THIS POINT IT would be helpful to look at some other reasons for suffering we may find in the Bible as well as some more questionable reasons often put forward as having their sources in the Bible.

Just Punishment

We have touched on one explanation for suffering which we see in the Hebrew scripture which compliments the Recipient Oriented Theodicy, even though it is sometimes so dominant that the other is often ignored or forgotten. The Hebrew scripture is filled with examples of individuals as well as entire nations who are punished for their evil actions (e.g., an evil city like Sodom, Gen 18:20–24; or the nation of Judah, 2 Chr 36:15–16). With the Mosaic Covenant, God told the Israelites that if they keep his laws, he will protect and prosper them. On the other hand, extreme suffering will come if God is rejected and the law disregarded (Deut 28:1–2, 15). It was often assumed that if suffering comes, it is because of some sin in one's life. Jesus' disciples, for example, assumed this of those who suffer (John 9:1–2). Job's friends repeatedly accused him of sin because such great suffering had come upon him.

Thus both principles are often seen in biblical times both in the Hebrew scripture as well as in the New Testament. Jesus had to make it clear that suffering was not always a result of sin (see his response in the last passage mentioned above, John 9:3). However, he also acknowledged that sometimes it was a result of one's sin (Luke 13:1–5). Christian and Jewish thought has always been aware that suffering was allowed for reasons other than punishment and justice. It was especially allowed for the purpose of testing our response to God, as the book of Job tells us.

Fall Theodicies

Another reason for suffering which many have seen in the scripture comes from the Genesis account of the fall, the first entrance of sin in the world. Adam and Eve's disobedience to God by eating the fruit of the tree of the knowledge of good and evil, as the story tells us, is the basic reason for death and certain forms of suffering in the world. The apostle Paul writes that death came to humanity because of Adam's sin and with this he also emphasizes that all people sin (Rom 5:12–19). Indeed, more than merely the specific suffering, subjugation, and death mentioned in Genesis 3, some would claim that all the suffering we face originated with the fall. The suffering Adam and Eve received for their sin may be what they deserved, but it is more difficult to understand how this could be an appropriate punishment for all of their descendants.

Adam and Eve as the First Humans

As something of a side note, let me say something about the historicity of the Genesis creation account and whether there actually existed a first human couple, Adam and Eve, from whom all people originated. After I do this we will endeavor to understand how or whether their first sin could bring sin and suffering to their descendants.

Henri Blocher calls the Genesis creation story prose-poetry. John Collins calls it exalted prose. This kind of assessment from such prominent biblical scholars would lead us to think it should be interpreted much as we would poetic literature. If we see this as poetic literature, this does not mean it can be made to say anything we want it to say. The creation story must in some important ways correspond with what actually happened.

The Genesis account is given in an agrarian setting; Adam was to tend the garden in Eden. Agriculture came into being around ten thousand years ago. The original events could have occurred in a gatherer culture with the story altered to eventually fit the agrarian culture when it came into being. God would have simply made sure that with the oral transmission of the story, the important truths he wanted remembered would remain.

PART I: HUMAN SUFFERING, THE GREATEST PROBLEM FOR BELIEF IN GOD

Population geneticists tell us that there never was a time that less than a few thousand of our species existed at once. I believe the currently accepted number is about ten thousand. If that is the case, how could there exist just two humans from whom all others originated?

For new species to originate, one individual has a mutation or the last of a number of mutations which has some survival benefit and that individual produces offspring some of whom carry on that beneficial mutation. The mutation produces a survival advantage. Sometimes the rest of the species perish since they lack that advantage and cannot compete for resources. At other times they become separated from those with that advantage and, lacking that competition, may survive.

One individual of an interbreeding population of non-human bipedal primates had the mutation which made it human. Thus we start with one individual producing a new subspecies which further interbreeds with others of both the old and new subspecies but the new eventually displaces the old. This is how we can have one originating human within a large interbreeding population of non-humans.

To have two originating humans, a first couple, we need add only minor developments to this scenario. Without getting into those details, and there are several possible variations on this scenario, we should see that there is no problem having a first originating couple as the Genesis account and the New Testament tell us. We have the first humans living and interbreeding with non-humans of their species until the non-human subspecies dies out.

I do not want to spend more time on this issue since it is so distant from the topic at hand. For those who would like to look into this further, I would recommend the reference in this footnote.[1]

This takes us back to the story of the fall. We see that there could have been an original human couple who fell into sin and somehow affected

---

1. The one of several possible scenarios I think would be most likely is discussed in William Lane Craig's Forum section of his *Reasonable Faith* web site under the topic "The Greatest Scientific Problem," http://www.reasonablefaith.org/forums/choose-your-own-topic/the-greatest-scientific-problem-christianity-6032144.0.html. The entire discussion is very long and some participants have taken it very far from the original opening presentation (the OP) to topics like the origin of life and evidence for and against evolution. The basic scenario is covered in the OP on page 1 and some tentative concluding statements in Reply (hereafter R) 162 and 163 on page 11. For those wishing to follow the discussion in more detail but without reading the whole thread, rabbit trails and all, I would suggest the following: OP, R7, 16, 18, 20–22, 24, 32, 53, 55, 56, 64, 66, 68, 83, 85, 98, 109, 114, 115, 119, 121, 123, 125 (pp. 1–9); R162, 163 (p. 11); R217–27 (pp. 15–16).

their descendants, those of the new subspecies. We can now look at how or whether the story of the fall relates to evil and suffering in the world.

Federal View

One widely accepted view of the fall which largely developed from John Calvin's theology says that Adam is our federal head; as our representative he made the choice of evil, disobeying God, rather than the good choice of obeying God. (Many Calvinists will also say that even Adam's choice was not free, but that's a different problem we cannot get into in this study.) As our representative, Adam did this in our place and we are guilty of his sin. We rightly deserve any suffering we receive, this position claims, since he chose for us.

This view faces some very serious difficulties however. How can we be guilty or deserving of the punishment of our representative when we never chose him as our representative? Imagine being taken to court for a crime someone else has committed. When you ask why you should be considered responsible for his act, you are told that the court had decided he should be your representative and whatever he chooses will be considered your choice. I think any reasonable person should see this view as absurd. Even if it is God who says one is guilty for another person's sin, this cannot make it so (so in fact, God could never say this). One cannot be guilty and deserving of punishment under such a doctrine and it provides no good explanation for the suffering in the world. (I would not want to say that there can be no conditions under which one may take another's guilt or sin. But there needs to be the willing choice to do so.)

Realistic Imputation

Another possible explanation for the reason all people sin and for the existence of evil involves a view of the fall which largely originated with Augustine. It says that all of Adam's descendants are *in Adam* in some realistic sense. Not only is a part of Adam passed on to us genetically or physically, but the choice Adam made is passed on as a part of us. More accurately, this part of Adam, this choice to disobey God, *we had each actually made* since we are in some sense a part of Adam. In this particular point of choice, *we are* Adam. For one person to sin and for God to create numerous others who possess that sin as part of themselves, God would be creating those

PART I: HUMAN SUFFERING, THE GREATEST PROBLEM FOR BELIEF IN GOD

people to be guilty of his sin and deserving of punishment. It would almost be as if God created humanity by dividing Adam into numerous other individuals. This is called realistic imputation of sin or realistic or seminal union with Adam.

However, the process of God creating each of us as distinct persons from Adam carrying his sin and guilt also carries with it an obligation on God's part. By essentially creating a hundred and five billion guilty Adams (the number of people who have existed) from one guilty couple, God was multiplying the number of people who deserve to receive punishment. God was not obligated to offer forgiveness to Adam and Eve who originally chose to disobey God since they had both freely chosen to sin. But by creating more creatures who deserve the punishment of Adam and Eve by inheriting their choice to sin, God would be obligated to offer a means by which they could be absolved of their guilt—which, indeed, the Bible tells us God has done: God has consigned all to disobedience so that God may have mercy on all (Rom 11:32).

Much sin creates suffering and any sin someone has freely committed deserves punishment. Much suffering may then be a result of one's sin, whether our original inherited sin or the sins we freely commit in each of our lives. Those who receive forgiveness of sin will have the pain they receive, that is, the punishment that results from this sin, compensated or negated. Remember that earlier we discussed how God compensates or even negates all undeserved suffering. God would do the same for forgiven sin. If our sins are forgiven, that must also include the original sin of Adam with which our lives are stained.

We can see ourselves as being created with Adam's sin and guilt and even deserving of any punishment that sin requires. But that punishment, that suffering, whether or not we actually deserve it, also serves the purpose of our testing. Whatever suffering we endure because of our identity in the fall of Adam serves to test us in the same manner as it does under the Recipient Oriented Theodicy. We are tested as to how we will respond to the God who allowed us this suffering.

In this realistic imputation view, everyone had committed the same original sin. Yet human suffering varies greatly from one person to another. Therefore much of our suffering cannot be accounted for by virtue of our having sinned in Adam. But neither can all of it be accounted for by suggesting that greater punishment befalls those who commit greater evil. We see very evil people often enduring little suffering and many good or

Other Biblical Answers

otherwise innocent people undergoing much suffering. Much of our suffering is undeserved.

We have to conclude that none of the fall oriented theodicies we have looked at have an adequate explanation for all of the suffering we find in the world. Realistic imputation of a sinful nature may explain how it is that everyone does sin at some time or another, but it does not adequately explain the existence of undeserved suffering.

4

Biblical Support for the Recipient Oriented Theodicy

LET ME BRING UP a sampling of scriptural passages which call for a Recipient Oriented Theodicy. I have first mentioned that this answer to the problem of suffering is the rationale we find in Job for his suffering (1:8–12; 2:3–6).

This testing is also the rationale behind God's command to Abraham to sacrifice his son Isaac (Gen 22:1–18). The Hebrew scriptures tell us that God abhors human sacrifice (Lev 18:21) and it tells us that God stopped Abraham just before he was about to kill his son; thus God never intended the act to be carried out. So God cannot be accused of even intending Isaac's death. Abraham knew that God had promised him that this son would carry on his line and become a great nation. So he knew that Isaac would either somehow not die or would be raised from the dead (as the writer of the book of Hebrews claims, 11:17–19). With this belief, Abraham would not have been guilty of the moral evil of killing his son had he done so. But more importantly for our concern, God needed to know if Abraham was willing to give up the one thing on earth he valued most, his very son. He was obedient to God in even the most extreme testing. Abraham was tested so that God could know whether he would freely choose the good of obeying God while enduring the pain of believing that his son would be killed, even if only temporarily. By his obedience to God, Abraham became good and pleasing to God in a way he never could have otherwise.

In Deuteronomy 13, God said that if a prophet makes predictions which come to pass (the normal means of knowing one is a true prophet according to Deut 18) but if they tell the people to follow other gods,

Biblical Support for the Recipient Oriented Theodicy

they are to judge this prophet to be a false prophet who would deserve to die. "Yahweh your God *is testing you to know whether you love* Yahweh your God with all of your heart and with all *of* your inner self," God says (13:3 LEB, italics in the original).

It is assumed that the Israelites already had good reason to believe that Yahweh was the true God but they are now facing strong counter-evidence against this belief. During the exodus, the Israelites had good reason to believe from the signs and wonders which were almost a daily occurrence (the parting of the Red Sea, the pillar of smoke by day and fire by night, manna from heaven, etc.) but after their time God would sometimes need to provide the people with other kinds of evidence.

Jesus and Paul would many centuries later talk about the witness of the Holy Spirit providing sufficient reason to believe (e.g., Matt 16:17; Eph 1:13–14; Rom 8:16). So this was likely also the Israelites' usual grounds for belief and for loving God when other miraculous evidence was not available. The Holy Spirit would draw the people to love and trust in God and would provided reason to believe, but this kind of reason was not necessarily so strong that it was unquestionable once confronted with stronger counter-evidence. By this kind of testing, God would know whether one would love God with all of one's heart; God would know what they would choose when the evidence for Yahweh's existence was perceived to be weaker than the evidence for disbelief.

C. S. Lewis points out that once we come to trust a person, we should no longer follow the old rule of proportioning our belief exactly according to the strength of the evidence as we perceive it.[1] Suppose a close friend is on trial for a crime and claims to be innocent. When we have come to deeply trust a person, the evidence against them must be absolute before we believe it. Likewise God was testing the Israelites to see if they would continue to trust in the God they had come to know and love even in the face of perceived stronger evidence to distrust or disbelieve in this God. God would then know whether one would love God with all of one's heart. Only if the evidence became so strong as to be undeniable should one give up this belief in Yahweh. Until then one should continue to trust this God. If one passes the test, God will eventually again give stronger evidence against the counter-evidence and provide sufficient reason to trust in Yahweh. As with so much of human testing, this kind of testing does not involve any obvious suffering as did Job's test. But it is the same kind of testing the

---

1. Lewis, "On Obstinacy in Belief," 13–30.

scripture so often mentions. By testing us God will know what our final choice will be and we become something different, something better, by making that choice.

I could point out more biblical examples. God tests us to know if we will cling to God when all else is taken from us. "If the fig tree does not bud," Habakkuk wrote, "and the vines produce no fruit, if the olive trees should fail or the fields bring forth no grain, still I will rejoice in the Lord, for the Lord is my strength" (3:17–19, abridged and paraphrased). God is said to have tested the Jewish king Hezekiah to discover what was in his heart when God allowed him to display his wealth to visiting Babylonian envoys (2 Chr 32:31). We are told that the Israelites were tested for forty years in the wilderness (Deut 8:2, 16) and Peter said that the testing of our faith refines it and results in our honor and glory (1 Pet 1:6–7). James speaks of the testing of our faith bringing about perseverance and maturity (Jas 1:2–4).

Without further explanation, some of these examples will sound as though God's testing is a very mechanical process: our testing through suffering just makes us better. But the process that brings about our progression must involve free choice, otherwise God could simply make us as good as God wants us to be without our going through that suffering. Only by freely choosing to be faithful to God as we respond to suffering can we become something more than God could make us without that free choice. If free choice were not involved and God merely wanted to know *what is in our hearts*, God could examine our hearts and minds without our making any decision.

John Schneider claims the Jobian theodicy is either "bad moral theology" or simply pointless sarcasm. He complains that God had no reason to take Satan's bet because it involved "ruining the life and family of a good man in the bargain," as if God would never restore such a loss.[2] And is such a loss even worth comparing to God's knowing the outcome of the test and our becoming something we could never otherwise become without the test? No. Admittedly the story does not allow for complete resolution if looked at literally rather than poetically. For example, Job's children and beloved servants were still lost to him. A more complete and realistic understanding of how God will completely restore all things and reconcile all things to himself was not to be revealed until the time of Jesus. Now we know that Job will either now or one day have his children back. So this is

---

2. Schneider, "Recent Genetic Science," 212n70, 71.

Biblical Support for the Recipient Oriented Theodicy

not sarcasm and it's ultimately a very good and powerful moral theology considering the enormous good that came of Job's testing.

Sean Carroll complains about the common theistic responses to the Problem of Evil: "It's not that [we should expect that] there should be no evil in the world if God exists, it's that you can always wriggle out of the prediction that there should be no evil in the world if God exists."[3] But it is not a matter of wriggling out of the prediction, it is rather that there is no good reason for the prediction. One wonders how Carroll would respond to this very basic Jobian theodicy. That one would expect only a world without suffering if God created it appears extremely shallow and simplistic. Atheists like Carroll seem to expect that if there is a God, we should imagine him as a fat, little Buddha-like figure who just sits there with his half-smile and closed eyes and wants everyone to love him and be happy. (And if we're happy enough we can probably forget about the part about loving him—unless that means nothing more than some token and distant acknowledgement.) He creates us to live our empty, er, happy little lives without suffering in our happy little homes with our happy little families. We schmooze with our happy little friends and our happy and somewhat shallow little brains think "It can't get any better than this."

This is hardly the God of the Bible. The biblical God is a God who created conscious moral agents who possess the dignity to create themselves as good or evil by their free choice in the face of suffering, a God who wanted more than mere machines who might be determined by God to do only good. This is the God who by this means brought about a far greater good than could be achieved by any other means. This is the God who wanted more than just empty little people living their painless, empty little lives for really no reason at all. And those who think that "it can't get any better than this" for their shallow, animal-like existence have not even reached the level of a truly human rationality. God has planted eternity in our hearts, and if we are honest with ourselves, we can never be content until we leave mere existence far behind us. This is the God who created us to know the greatest of all joys, the joy of knowing God. But this God also wanted us to come to know him by our strong decision and often within the harsh and strafing environment of suffering.

---

3. Craig vs. Carroll; Carroll, first rebuttal, par. 9.

5

Foreknowledge and the Testing Theodicies

THERE ARE GENERALLY FOUR theistic views of divine foreknowledge which in some ways either support or deny the Recipient Oriented Free Will Theodicy and other testing theodicies.[1] A common *Calvinistic* view would say that God foreknows whatever will happen because God has determined that it should happen. What we take to be free decisions are instead completely determined by God to be exactly what God chooses them to be. (I will call this view simply Calvinism.) *Molinism* says that God foreknows all that will happen including all future free choices. For the Molinist, free decisions are not determined by God but by the individual making the choice. This would be libertarian free will. But Molinism says God also knows what free choices everyone would make even if they never in fact make them. The *simple foreknowledge* view says that God knows all that will happen in the future, including free choices, but not the decisions people would make but never have the opportunity to do so. The theological position called *open theism* would say that God cannot know future free choices at all until they occur. God does however know future events which result from normal causally determined processes.

The open theist view more readily fits the passages we have looked at than any of the other views. God has Satan test Job because he does not know what he will choose, how he will respond to God in the face

---

1. A more thorough presentation of the arguments of this chapter can be found at Jensen, "God's Foreknowledge." Beilby and Eddy (eds.), *Divine Foreknowledge: Four Views* goes into an even more detailed analysis of many of the arguments for and against the four views considered.

Foreknowledge and the Testing Theodicies

of suffering, until Job makes his decision. On the other hand, the simple foreknowledge view would reread the account as suggesting that God did foreknow the outcome of Job's choices though God could not have this knowledge without Job enduring his test and making his decision in the context of his suffering. So Job's testing given the Recipient Oriented Free Will Theodicy can be understood under the simple foreknowledge view.

The other passages I have brought up also fit the simple foreknowledge view though the more obvious meaning of these passages must be sacrificed. God was not actually waiting to see what Job or Abraham or Hezekiah or the tested Israelite would do; God knew but God did so by seeing the future events occur. Also, God used these tests to allow these people to become good in a way they never could by any other means. As with open theism, God needed to know what they would choose and they needed to become good by making that choice.

My point is that though it is possible to read all of the passages we have looked at with a simple foreknowledge understanding, the open theist understanding is more natural and obvious. Only in Genesis 22 when God honors Abraham and tells him "now I know that you fear God" does the simple foreknowledge view appear even more strained and unlikely. Open theism is much more likely.

The simple foreknowledge understanding as well as the open theist view, both of which reject Molinism, answer a common criticism of the Jobian theodicy. Job's God is sometimes depicted as someone who had no good reason to take up Satan's bet since God "knew the outcome in advance."[2] Under simple foreknowledge, the event has to occur to be foreknown. Under open theism, God did not know the outcome in advance. So in both cases, the free choice had to be made for the outcome to be known.

A Molinist form of the Recipient Oriented Theodicy is possible though it falls prey to the above criticism. It says significantly less than the open theist or simple foreknowledge forms and it is more difficult to read into most of the passages we have looked at. How can God appear to desire to know Job's response to God in his suffering if God already knows without having any suffering occur? How can God say that now he knows Abraham fears God if God already knew beforehand without his having to endure the test? How can the Israelites or Hezekiah be tested as to what moral choices they will make if God already knew what they would be without the test occurring? Molinism would say not that God needs to *find out* what

---

2. Schneider, "Recent Genetic Science," 212n70.

Part I: Human Suffering, The Greatest Problem for Belief in God

decision we will make in the face of suffering; rather, it says only that it is most important that our free choice to be faithful to our creator in the face of suffering occurs. This free choice to be faithful to God makes us good in a way we could not otherwise become.

The Calvinist view ill fits the Recipient Oriented Free Will Theodicy more than any of the others we have looked at. God does not need or want to find out what choice we will make since God has already determined what that should be. The passages we have looked at are also less compatible with Calvinism than any other view of foreknowledge. Even Molinism has the individual freely choose as they endure their testing. For the Molinist, God knows our future free choices even if we never make them, or for that matter, even if we are never brought into existence to make them. Nevertheless, under Molinism God did want to know what those free choices would be which determine our final moral condition and our relationship with God. For the Calvinist, no free moral choice occurs at all since God has fully determined how we will respond. Since we have no real choice, our choices cannot matter to God. The closest the Calvinist view could come to supporting a Recipient Oriented Free Will Theodicy would be to say that Job's (predestined) moral choice to stay faithful to God in the face of suffering makes him morally better in some inexplicable manner.

Certain scriptural passages such as Jesus' prediction of Peter's denial or Judas's betrayal of Jesus are sometimes taken as proof-texts demonstrating that the Bible indicates that God knows our future free choices (John 6:70–71; Matt 26:21–25, 47; Mark 14:27–31, 66–72). But to adequately evaluate these passages we need to consider that many moral choices may be determined by one's prior choices. A person may make a free moral choice at one or several times in one's life which they hold to so strongly that they are unable to later make a different decision. Paul speaks of God eventually giving people over to their evil desires as they continually refuse God's drawing and calling (Rom 1:21–25, 28–32). Because God patiently calls all people to himself to forsake their sins (Rom 2:4; 2 Pet 3:9) God would not hand them over to be bound by their desires until they have reached that extreme limit. Some may not necessarily reach a point of full reprobation while they may still be unable to make a free choice of a certain type. Since this could easily be what occurred with Peter, Judas, Pilate, and others, their examples do not provide adequate biblical grounds for belief in divine foreknowledge of free choices. One may thus be responsible for a choice though unable to choose otherwise. In my essay "God's Foreknowledge" I believe I have demonstrated that no other passages provide good reason to claim the Bible teaches that God foreknows free choices.

Our current conclusion is that the Recipient Oriented Free Will Theodicy, especially in its stronger form, has persuasive support throughout the Bible. Again, the stronger form is that God tests us to know what our decisions will be and that we become good in a way we could not become otherwise when we freely affirm our commitment to God in the face of suffering.

6

The Problem of Lost Loved Ones

THE READER MAY NOTICE a special problem which arrises with the problem of suffering as applied to the loss of a child. The Recipient Oriented Theodicy basically applies to the parent who endures this loss. It says that they will have the child back some day and the real testing involves being willing to wait and to accept God's decision to take this life. God tests us to determine how we will respond to God in the face of suffering. The Bible says that the bereaved parent who passes the test will have the child back and they will be together for eternity. The undeserved suffering of both parent and child occurs for a reason and will be infinitely compensated. This is true if both the parent and (eventually) the child accept God and God's plan for them and are thus accepted by God. But what if one or both do not accept God or God's plan for them? How can someone endure eternal separation from those they love?

Now obviously our problem does not necessarily involve only a parent and child. It applies to any person who loves *anyone* else—parent-child, husband-wife, friend-friend, etc.—and it applies whether either loved one has died prematurely or not. For simplicity sake I will continue to present the problem as involving the loss of a child.

Before looking at this problem, we should have a clear understanding of the several possible theological views of the afterlife and some terms I will be using. I will select from a broad spectrum of theological views in order to include those which are relevant to the issues raised here as well as those which claim to closely follow from biblical teaching.

The Problem of Lost Loved Ones

Most biblical theologies claim that there are people who are rejected by God in the next life, whether permanently or only temporarily, whom we may call the *lost*. Those who temporarily or never experience this time of afterlife separation from God and who are ultimately fully accepted by God, I will call the *redeemed*. Thus the lost may become the redeemed in some views. *Hell* is then a permanent or temporary place or state of punishment or purging for the lost. Some Christian theologies hold that the lost are those who have adamantly and finally rejected God and God's offer of reunion with God and who can never have reconciliation with God. In some other views they will eventually become the redeemed. In still others they will eventually be reconciled to God but lack the full completeness and possibly the full relationship with God the redeemed possess.

By *eternalism* I mean belief in eternal conscious torment (ECT) for the lost. All immediately enter heaven given *simple universalism* and will never be lost, but under *restorationist universalism* (sometimes shortened to *restorationism*) the lost must first suffer punishment or purging for a limited amount of time before being accepted by God. Restorationist universalism would thus espouse a kind of temporary hell such as I have mentioned above. *Annihilationism* says that the lost will be extinguished, though usually it will claim this occurs after some time of punishment.[1]

Now back to the problem of lost loved ones. Suppose both parent and child finally reject God and God's offer of reunion with God. Under eternalism, annihilationism, and some forms of restorationist universalism, if there is any possibility that they will have reunion with each other in hell, they will have no joy in the meeting and there will be no love one for the other so long as they are in hell.

One of the first things we should notice in dealing with this problem for the non-universalist views, including some forms of restorationism, is that any continued suffering is entirely a result of human choice. The initial suffering, the loss of the child, fulfills God's purpose and will be compensated if the parent and child fulfill their moral responsibility to God and each other. So God offers a way that the suffering from the loss of a beloved child may be recompensed or redeemed. In the non-universalist views, if both

---

1. Some of the terms used here are simply the terms I prefer. "Eternalism," for example, is more commonly called "traditionalism." But eternalism seems to me a more appropriate and intuitively correct term. "Conditional immortality" is a more popular form of annihilationism and it is the more commonly used term. But because the term "annihilationism" is simpler and more general, and more obvious for those who are new to this discussion, I will use this term to designate any belief in extinction of consciousness.

refuse this offer, it is their own fault for allowing this suffering to continue and for not taking the full good, the recompense, God offers them. An undeserved suffering that could have been negated or nullified can become a deserved suffering that will not be negated.

Suppose one person is faithful to God and the other is not. Doesn't the faithful one have to suffer too? How can God "wipe away every tear" of the redeemed (Rev 21:4) if a loved one is eternally separated from them or annihilated, or even worse, if they are to endure eternal torment? This is one of the most difficult issues the Christian will ever face. This is not only a problem for those redeemed who happen to have lost loved ones. I would argue that an adequate doctrine of the love of God must maintain that when the redeemed have learned to love as God loves, all of the lost will be lost loved ones for them. Indeed, how can God be content if even one person is eternally destroyed or alienated from God? God's love for the lost will always be far greater than that of the redeemed.

If one individual, the parent or child, is lost, I believe that for God to wipe away all tears requires a universalism of some form. Neither annihilationism nor eternalism can adequately mitigate the anguish of the redeemed who have lost loved ones. A common eternalist and annihilationist response is that in paradise God will remove the memory of the lost loved one. This position is simply unacceptable. Paradise becomes a place of eternal deception and ignorance. This is something paradise simply cannot be for those who are fully accepted by God.

The horror of this problem becomes overwhelming if we might imagine that eternalism were true. Imagine the lost enduring eternal torment while the redeemed experience eternal bliss simply because they have no memory of their lost loved ones. I cannot see how anyone can consider this solution to be acceptable. Only a form of universalism can resolve this problem. Under the various forms of universalism, the lost will at worst only temporarily endure conscious suffering and separation from their redeemed loved ones and from God.

An even more serious problem is one I have discussed in the book *Flirting with Universalism* but can touch on only briefly here. It can be expressed by the question, "How can an intrinsically good God allow eternal conscious suffering for anyone?" This problem reduces to an awareness that this is something a good God simply cannot do. Universalism does resolve this problem. Annihilationism may adequately answer this problem though it leaves us with other difficulties. Eternalism, I would claim, definitely cannot answer this problem.

Our two problems again, addressed as questions, are "How can a good God allow eternal suffering, ECT, for anyone?" and "How can God wipe away all tears of the redeemed?" Restorationism says God does not allow ECT and that when all of the lost are redeemed, then all tears will be wiped away. Not all forms of universalism, including all forms of restorationism, can claim to be consistent with scriptural teaching, our human awareness of goodness and justice, or our awareness of our need to honor one's right to determine one's own fate. In *Flirting with Universalism* I argue that a particular form of restorationist universalism, *semi-restorationism,* can adequately answer both of these problems while remaining ethically satisfying and true to biblical teaching.[2]

To allay a possible confusion, I need to say just a little more about this particular view. Semi-restorationism says that some have and will finally reject God and God's offer of salvation and will endure a time of pain and punishment proportionate to all of the evil they have committed. Yet in the end God cannot allow any to know the greatest of all pain, the pain eternal separation from God entails. The lost will eventually be reconciled to God, even if this ultimately involves removing their ability to freely choose against God. They will know the fulfillment only God's love and presence can give, though possibly they will not possess the same full and complete joy experienced by those who have willingly chosen to embrace God and his will. They may lack other capacities as well. Though they will not be aware of it, they will be marked with the stigma of having rejected their God and Father. As Revelation 14:11 tells us, the smoke or memorial of their (past) torment ascends forever. Many past memories will also be removed. Eternal ignorance in this case is not eternal deception. This will all be part of the final and eternal *painless* punishment of the lost.

The reader may notice that throughout this book I have sometimes spoken of the lost as being eternally judged and punished by God and at other times as being redeemed by God to experience eternal joy. This is the possible confusion I alluded to earlier. The lost can be said to endure a kind of eternal punishment while still experiencing the joy of knowing God. So we see that both are possible.

2. Christian history includes several similar *half universalist* views (e.g., John Scotus Eriugena), if I might call them that. Stephen Williams offers an interesting look at similar views from the last two centuries in "Is there a Fourth View?" 263–83. (Thanks to Matt Marston for pointing me to Williams's essay.)

Part I: Human Suffering, The Greatest Problem for Belief in God

We do have our answer to the main question of this chapter: all forms of universalism would resolve the problem of lost loved ones. The issue which must be dealt with elsewhere is whether any form of universalism is sufficiently compatible with our moral awareness and biblical teaching. Again, I believe at least one particular form of restorationist universalism is.

7

The Observer Oriented Free Will Theodicy

ANOTHER REASON THE BIBLE gives for undeserved suffering, like losing a child, is that God wants to know how we, as outside observers, will react to others' suffering. When we see images of starving children on our televisions and we are asked to help, will we do something? Will we harden our hearts or will we let compassion grow within us? God wants to know if we will learn to have God's heart. It may be by doing as little as sending money or as much as dedicating one's life to medicine or agriculture or some other appropriate technology to help people. One may come to have God's compassion by simply being available when a friend or neighbor is facing a hardship and they need someone to talk with. God wants to know how we will respond to others in their suffering and if we will choose the good and become good in the way God wants us to become. God allows some evils so that a greater good may occur by means of our choice and our actions in response to those evils. This would be called the Observer Oriented Free Will Theodicy.

I mentioned that the problem of child suffering basically involves a Recipient Oriented Theodicy for the parents in that this loss produces for them true emotional suffering. Some of our greatest suffering involves our anguish over the suffering of those we love. Technically, however, it may be called an Observer Oriented Theodicy insofar as the parent is responding to the suffering of someone else. When we have a less natural attachment to the person suffering, we can more easily or clearly recognize that the theodicy involved would be observer oriented.

PART I: HUMAN SUFFERING, THE GREATEST PROBLEM FOR BELIEF IN GOD

We must understand that a grave responsibility is placed upon our shoulders as we witness the pain of others. By our choice we become either more like God or we lose something of our humanness; we embrace God's deep compassion for those in pain or we anesthetize ourselves morally. God wants us to have his heart, to love good and hate evil, to feel the anguish God feels when mistreatment and injustice is done. God wants us to do all that we can to stop the evil we see.

This particular approach suggests that whatever the reasons there must be some suffering and pain on earth, much of it need not be as great should we intervene. The examples I have just mentioned demonstrate this. The holocaust would be another example. It may have been necessary that some greater than normal suffering occur at this time in history, but it could have been much less for many or possibly even all of the victims. If a German Christian had put aside her fear and hid a Jewish family, if her Christian brother living in another country who knew about the genocide took the time to pray for the holocaust victims, if we all just did what we were supposed to do and could do, the horror of the holocaust would have been so much less.

In Christianity God desires that we pray because this shows our desire and longing for that which God desires. Because God wants to know that we have the same longing, the same anguish of soul in many cases, and because God wants us to be people who have this longing, often God will not act to remedy a wrong unless we first feel and express that desire ourselves. And of course, God sometimes has other reasons for not answering our prayer as we request. Sometimes the test or trial must be endured no matter how much we may pray to remove it.

Soul Strength and Suffering

The variation in the amount of suffering people endure is determined in part by God's knowledge of how much they are able to endure. Like the brighter students in a class who are given harder assignments and exams so that they will achieve more, so God gives the stronger souls harder tests so that they will achieve more by passing the test. Paul tells us that God allows no one to be tempted beyond what they can endure (1 Cor 10:13). In Acts 17:26–27 Paul indicates that God allows people to be born at the times and locations which are most conducive to their salvation, presumably according to how spiritually strong or weak God creates them. One's spiritual strength is also determined in part by one's own decisions. According to one's soul strength God also determines what later life situations one will face. Weaker souls may not be allowed to endure a Nazi concentration camp, for example. (Note that one's ostensive reactions when enduring such suffering do not necessarily indicate the actual moral strength or weakness of the individual.)

For many people then, God allows an upper limit of pain that would vary with the individual according to what they can endure. Below that upper limit, there could be a great degree of variation. Here we may see that the Observer Oriented Free Will Theodicy would suggest that up to that limit God may allow one very great suffering if Christians and non-Christians do not fulfill their responsibilities (aid, prayer, counsel, comfort, protection, etc.) or God may allow one far less suffering if Christians and non-Christians do fulfill their responsibilities before God.

If we think of a world created for the purposes described in the Observer and Recipient Oriented Theodicies, we can also imagine that it could include the changes our actions would produce, actions such as our intercession and involvement to create less suffering. But such a world need not be observably distinguishable from a purely naturalistic world filled with somewhat random occurrences of pain. People can hide Jewish families during a holocaust given a purely naturalistic world as much as they can in a theistic world (one which includes a God who created everything other than God). If many people pray to eliminate some evil and that evil ends, we may be able to attribute this result as easily to chance as to divine intervention. But in some cases it will appear to be unlikely that the elimination of that evil could occur by pure chance. In those cases we would have evidence of a theistic or supernatural world.

The Observer Oriented Theodicy in the Bible

The Observer Oriented Free Will Theodicy is strongly evident in the New Testament. Jesus taught that the Kingdom of God advances when the sick are healed, the oppressed delivered, the captive released (Luke 4:18–19; Matt 11:2–5). The writer of John's first epistle said that Jesus' command was to love each other and that God's love does not dwell in those who do not allow compassion and pity to move them to act when they see someone in need (1 John 3:11, 17–18). Jesus said that a particular man was born blind so that God's works or glory would be displayed by his healing (John

9:2–3). God is glorified and God's will is done when good is done, when one seeks to have God's heart and to aid the suffering. He said that his followers will be sons and daughters of their Father, God, as they love their enemies and pray for those who persecute them (Matt 5:44–45) and as they seek to remove strife and violence (5:9). The Judge of all the earth will condemn or honor us according to how we respond to those of least importance, how we let compassion motivate us or how we fail to let it motivate us to act. How will we respond to the oppressed? Will we aid, feed, protect, clothe, shelter, care for, or comfort the hungry, the imprisoned, the homeless, the stranger, the sick, the cold, or the naked (25:31–40)? God wants us to have this compassion in us because this is God's heart.

Notice that this teaching is deeply engrained in the Hebrew scripture as well as in Jesus' teachings. This is a God who has compassion on the suffering and is distraught when the wicked must be judged (e.g., Exod 2:24–25; Jer 31:20; Ezek 33:11). God desires us to care for the weak and needy and abused because God hates oppression and mistreatment (Isa 1:16–17; Job 31:9–23, 29–34, 38–40; Mic 6:8). God allows us to live in a world in which oppression and mistreatment can occur to see if we will hate it as God hates it and fight to eliminate it. We become good in a way we could not become otherwise when we freely choose to hate and oppose evil as God does.

8

Salvation for the Unborn

THE RECIPIENT ORIENTED FREE Will Theodicy answers the problem of child suffering and death for the parents. The Observer Oriented Free Will Theodicy often answers this problem as well for those less attached to the suffering child. By means of the child's suffering, God sees the choice a very attached loved one or a less attached observer will make. They make the choices that will allow them to pass or fail important moral tests. Probably more often for the recipient of suffering than the outside observer, the moral choice involves questions of how they will respond or react to God for allowing such suffering.

Neither theodicy answers the problem for the child who has endured this pain. Children, at least if they are too young, will have no ability to face this suffering as a testing of their faith, as a means of deciding whether they will choose to trust in or reject God in the face of this suffering.

On the unusual chance that a child's death or suffering affects no outside observer or no one emotionally close to the child, this would possibly be a gratuitous evil. Its only justification would be that its possibility is an inevitable part of a larger world which itself is needed for other theodicies to play out and for greater goods to thus occur. But even if it is a gratuitous evil, it is very important to remember that the child's undeserved suffering is compensated and thus essentially negated.

Nevertheless, we should recognize that this cannot be the end of the story for the child. The child must be allowed the opportunity to have their own life of testing and decision making. Though the theodicies we have looked at provide reasons for the child's suffering, the child must be more than merely a means for some other person's testing.

I do not think the problem is resolved by saying that the child gets to go immediately to heaven with all undeserved suffering compensated. The child, like everyone else, needs to be tested; to endure the suffering required by the Recipient Oriented Free Will Theodicy; to choose to accept or reject God and not simply be ushered into heaven, no questions asked. Otherwise if God has no qualm about allowing some a life without testing and choice, however short it may be, why wouldn't God do this for everyone? The testing God allows us will certainly vary in kind and intensity from one person to another, but the scripture seems clear that all people must endure some amount of testing (e.g., Luke 17:1; 1 Thess 3:3–4).

The Bible teaches that all who enter paradise who are fully accepted by God are such because of certain choices they make—most significantly, their choice to accept God's proffered gift of salvation through Jesus Christ (John 3:3, 18; 11:25–26). To make a special exception, to say that some are given this kind of eternal life without being given such a choice, flies in the face of this most important biblical principle. Those who receive God's complete salvation can only have it because it is freely chosen, not because it is forced upon them.

There is an interesting implication to the belief that those who die too young go directly to heaven. Wouldn't Christians have to admit that physicians who perform abortions or child molesters who kill their victims are our most effective evangelists? Even if God does condemn abortion and infanticide, shouldn't Christians who believe in heaven and hell be happy to think that there can be no possibility that this child might be damned? Do many Christians unwittingly suppress a smile beneath their tears when they hear abortion statistics?

There is a related social consequence of this belief as well which is even more troubling. Sadly, there have been mentally unstable Christians who have killed their children in the belief that this would assure their salvation. Happily, this is very rare. Yet the possibility that some believers would be willing to do such an evil, even if they believed it would cost them their own souls, is also a logical consequence of this belief. Christians should certainly grieve over such a horrible action and loss just as they grieve over the unnecessary loss of other innocent children.

Of course, unstable atheists (and maybe some not so unstable) will sometimes commit equally horrendous evils. Remember Jeffrey Dahmer's statement that he felt no need to alter his behavior if he believed God did not exist.[1] (We will talk more about the moral consequences of religion vs. secularism in a later chapter. Dahmer, for those who may not know, was an American serial killer who committed rape, murder, and dismemberment on seventeen men and boys. Necrophilia and cannibalism were involved in some of the later murders.) Whatever the outcome, we must also not forget that beneficial or harmful social consequences do not determine truth. We must seek the truth by rational investigation independently of and even in spite of any practical results that follow the beliefs we consider.

Getting back to our main question, we are concerned about the miscarried and aborted fetus (when God has made it human) and the child who has died too young to have made any moral choices, and especially the ultimate moral choice of rejecting or accepting God and God's will for them. Possibly there are some who are mentally handicapped who are in this same category. This person must be given another opportunity to make that decision if they cannot do so in this life. But furthermore, this person must also be given sufficient time to make this choice in the context of a life that has some degree of suffering.

It may be that God has prepared another world much like our own to allow such persons a chance after death to make those morally significant decisions. It must be like ours in having not too much or too little evidence for God's existence. Because some people would feel constrained to believe or disbelieve and would not be able to freely choose for God or against God (whichever the case may be), the evidence cannot be too strong either way.

God may occasionally allow overwhelming or undeniable evidence but only when God has providentially provided that some individuals not witness it or adequately evaluate it. Those who are intellectually honest who have not yet decided for or against commitment to God may be in this category. If God is looking for their free decision to affirm or reject allegiance to God, God would not want the evidence to be too strong that God is there and deserves one's commitment, or that one will face judgment for willfully rejecting God. God would want their commitment to be based on their knowledge that this is something they ought to do, that this is what God deserves if God exists.

On the other hand, those who have already believed on weaker but adequate evidence or those who have professed a willingness to seek God and will to do God's will (as per John 7:17) may sometimes be given such

---

1. "Jeffrey Dahmer," Wikipedia.

undeniable evidence. Likewise, those who have closed their minds to accepting any possible evidence may also be allowed to witness it since no amount of evidence will influence them (Rom 1:28).

My own suspicion is that God will allow children who have died prematurely to return to a life in this world. Often Christians reject this claim or the claim that some will be reborn in any other similar world because the book of Hebrews says that it is appointed to humans to die *once* and after that to face God's judgment (9:27). But this passage does not apply to children or others before they make any choices which could affect how they will be judged or their final relationship with God. It only applies to those who have lived long enough to make such decisions and to make them in the face of some degree of suffering. Those who face God's judgment must have done something in this life to deserve judgment. They must also have the opportunity to freely choose to receive reconciliation with God.

Also, the Hebrews passage cannot be saying that absolutely no one can die more than once since the Bible tells us that Elijah, Elisha, Jesus, Peter, and Paul all raised people from the dead. Those raised from the dead clearly died more than once. And then there are at least a couple of people, Enoch and Elijah, who very possibly have not died even once. So there are some very obvious exceptions to this statement in Hebrews. Those who have died too young would be a similar exception to this rule. The passage merely means that *generally* those of the human race die no more nor less than once.

There are other obvious examples in scripture of general commands and statements which are not to be taken as unconditional or without exception. For example, we are told that we are to submit to and obey governing authorities (Rom 13:1–2; 1 Pet 2:13–14). Yet the scripture also tells us that if the state tells us to disobey God's commands, the state must be disobeyed (Acts 4:18–20). So the command to obey governing authorities is only generally binding on believers and is not without exception.

I have claimed that because God is absolutely good and just, God would not allow the creation of a fallen race without allowing them—*all* of them—the opportunity to be reconciled to God. Scripture clearly agrees with this obvious assumption. It was revealed to Peter that God does not show favoritism (Acts 10:34–35) and Paul also confirms this (Rom 2:11). This means that God does not arbitrarily show mercy to offer salvation to some but not to others. Even more pointedly, Paul writes, "For God has consigned *all* to disobedience, that he may have mercy on *all*" (Rom 11:32

SALVATION FOR THE UNBORN

RSV, italics added). God offers salvation to everyone. Thus all people must be given some minimal amount of time to make such a decision. Again, for those who die before they can make such a choice, this would have to occur by one's being reborn in this world or in another very much like it.

The reader may notice from the previous paragraphs claims that appear contradictory. I said that the Christian view is that all people must be given the opportunity to make the choice to accept God's offer of salvation. I also said that to be fully accepted by God one must accept God's gift of salvation by faith in Jesus Christ. But clearly, not everyone has or has had the opportunity to hear of Jesus in order to make this choice. To answer this and some related problems I would argue that all who seek God (John 7:17; Acts 17:27; Rom 10:13) and/or those who fear or reverence God and seek to do what is right (Acts 10:34–35) will find and accept the truth of Christianity. If they do not discover the truth of Christianity in this life, this must occur in the next.[2]

I need to here repeat and further discuss the answer to a problem we have discussed earlier. Some readers may feel confused if they recall that to answer some of the problems we have considered I had advocated a kind of universalism, that is, a view that everyone will eventually be reconciled to God. If this is so, how can I talk about the need to accept God's offer of salvation?

The universalism I advocate is a form of restorationism. All will be reconciled to God but only after a time of punishment for those who adamantly and finally reject God and his offer of salvation. For many people this will include merely rejecting every stimulus God gives them to motivate them to seek God. These are those who will bear the punishment their sins deserve. If we take Jesus' words seriously, that time of punishment is to be avoided at all costs. It would be better to cut off your hand or tear out your eye if that could keep you from that place of punishment (Mark 9:43–48). Even if it will someday end and even if that punishment is limited according to the amount of evil one has committed, it is still to be avoided by all possible means. Also, the particular form of restoration for which I have argued would say that even if everyone is eventually reconciled to God, there will still remain a kind of shame or stigma marking those who had finally and ultimately rejected their God.

---

2. For a more complete argument see chap. 8 of the previously mentioned book, Jensen, *Flirting with Universalism*.

Having said all of this I need to also make it clear that no doctrine of restorationism is in my thinking absolutely certain. I do think that the form of restorationism I hold to is more likely than any other view and I have argued that. Nevertheless, I cannot say that it is beyond any shadow of a doubt that some form of annihilationism cannot be true. I would never feel so confident about restorationism that I could ever assure someone that there can be no other alternative. The most fearful prospect that any honest reading of scripture would allow us to entertain is that after enduring whatever time of punishment the lost deserve, they will eventually cease to exist.

So whether annihilationism or restorationism is true, it is urgent that we consider and evaluate the Christian claims and call upon God for truth, if for no other reason than the sheer possibility that either is true. On the possibility that we could be rejecting our God and Creator and Source, that we may be refusing to accept the one channel God offers us by which our sins and the judgment they deserve can be removed—to refuse to honestly consider the Christian claims and seek the truth from God clearly would deserve God's judgment.

God desires to know how we will respond to him in the face of suffering. Our choices for or against God will determine whether and how God will accept or reject us even if all people are eventually reconciled to God. All people need a life that allows a sufficient amount of time to so respond to God. And we also need a life in which we make such decisions in the context of some degree of suffering.

9

The Insufficiency of the Agent and Observer Oriented Theodicies

WE HAVE CONSIDERED THE Recipient Oriented and the Observer Oriented Free Will Theodicies. What is commonly called simply *the* Free Will Theodicy is what I would here call the Agent Oriented Free Will Theodicy. Whether considered as a theistic defense or a theodicy, it essentially says that God allows us to freely choose to do evil because God wants us, as the agents of good or evil, to choose the good and be responsible for our choices. The possibility is left open that we may do evil since God cannot control our choice insofar as we are free. This is libertarian free will. We cannot be responsible for our actions unless we are free in this way. By being able to freely choose the good, a greater good would occur than if we were not free when we would so choose. It is better to freely choose even if one chooses evil than not to be able to freely choose at all. This basic concern for free choice is crucial to Recipient and Observer Oriented Theodicies as well.

Given the Agent Oriented Theodicy, much evil could occur and has occurred which God did and does not desire to occur. But even this kind of evil, as it affects the innocent, God is able to use to bring about good. It can still be used as undeserved suffering is used for the Recipient Oriented Theodicy. It would serve the purpose of testing the the victims' response to God.

But even so, God would rather not have anyone ever commit such evil. God would rather have the recipient of suffering receive any necessary undeserved pain through natural evil, from natural events and processes rather than human actions. Having the ability to freely choose good and evil is a greater good than not having this power at all. Also, once someone chooses to do good, they become good in a way they never could have without that choice.

If we had only the Observer Oriented or the Agent Oriented Theodicies, indeed, even if we had both but no Recipient Oriented Theodicy, we would not have an adequate response to the Problem of Evil. Even as mere theistic defenses, as hypothetical explanations for the Problem of Evil, they could not sufficiently answer the problem. Let me attempt to demonstrate this.

Suppose God's only reason for allowing evil is found in the rationale of the Agent Oriented Free Will Theodicy. Suppose God were merely concerned to see whether we would do good or evil—that is, inflict pain on others, refrain from doing so, or do good for others. Suppose God wants to know whether we will become good or evil by such choices (including our choices for or against God) without having to endure pain ourselves. Or, following the Observer Oriented Theodicy, suppose God wants to know if we will freely do good for those who are suffering and God wants us to become good through that free choice. Notice that in both cases we do not need to experience pain ourselves.

It is too easy to imagine that God could create us in a kind of dream world, or perhaps something like the computer simulation world of the *Matrix* movies. God could thus have us make our morally significant choices in a virtual world in which others do not actually exist and feel pain. We would honestly believe that we are inflicting pain or alleviating someone's suffering when in fact we are not. God would thus know what our choices would be and we would become good or evil by our free choice. And, more importantly, no one would be hurt in the process. In our present world other people definitely are hurt in the process. This dream world seems not only a possible world but also a feasible one God could create. Wouldn't a good God create a world in which the least possible amount of pain would occur insofar as the greatest good could also occur?

Would it make God a deceiver for God to create us in a dream world? Well, God created us in a world in which the sun appears to go around the earth, or at least travel through the sky from east to west. Does that also make God a deceiver? When we have dreams, at least when we have very vivid dreams, we often think at the time that the events are actually happening. If God created us to have such dreams, does this make God a liar? No, we were never promised at birth that everything we perceive is

The Insufficiency of the Agent and Observer Oriented Theodicies

truly as it appears. Many mistaken perceptions were meant to be correctly understood only after much thought and investigation (like the fact that the earth revolves around the sun). Usually we will eventually discover which phenomena do not correspond to the real world.

But the same would be true if we were created in a dream universe. If God eventually lets us know it is a dream world, there would be no evil in the deception. So God would likely create personal dream worlds for each of us if he only wanted to test us as to what pain we would cause or seek to alleviate in others and if God were not concerned that we should endure suffering ourselves.

Under the Agent and Observer Oriented Theodicies alone, just about the only suffering that God need require would be the anguish or discomfort one may feel in choosing to do evil or in thinking that someone else is suffering. Now one may also need to have some additional experience of pain oneself to be aware of the suffering one would be causing or alleviating. Still, for each person to experience just that much suffering would amount to far less pain than the world now appears to contain. So if God wanted only to test us as to how we would respond to others who suffer or to see if we would harm or do good for others, God could have created us in a virtual world with very little actual pain. And by that testing we could become good in a way we could not become otherwise.

The Recipient Oriented Theodicy does require suffering and, as we have seen, much more than the Observer and Agent Oriented Theodicies alone would require. The Recipient Oriented Theodicy says that *we* need to experience suffering, and sometimes very great suffering, that allows us to be tested. It tells us that we need the kind of suffering that we find in the world. Since we can see that we need this kind of world given the Recipient Oriented Theodicy, the Agent and Observer Oriented Theodicies can also fulfill their purpose in such a world. No special dream world need be created for them.

10

Summary

UNDER THE SIMPLE INSIGHT that we should not expect to know an omniscient God's reasons for allowing some evils for a greater good to occur, skeptical theism is capable of fully answering the Problem of Evil for belief in God. The Agent Oriented Free Will Theodicy or Theistic Defense is also valuable when used with the Recipient and Observer Oriented Free Will Theodicies. The Agent Oriented Theodicy looks at the agent of moral choices to do good or harm to others. The Recipient Oriented Theodicy looks at a person's response to God in the context of their suffering. The Observer Oriented Theodicy looks at one's response to the suffering of others.

Both the Observer and Agent Oriented Theodicies need the Recipient Oriented Theodicy to work. The Recipient and the Observer Oriented Theodicies are very powerful biblical answers to the most basic and disturbing aspects of the Problem of Evil. They answer these problems in a more emotionally satisfying manner than skeptical theism alone can do. They specifically answer certain of the most important aspects of the problem of child suffering. Other theodicies or defenses resolve other aspects of the Problem of Evil.

For example, the problem of lost loved ones asks how the redeemed in paradise can have joy knowing any of their loved ones are lost and separated from God. I believe this can only be adequately answered by some form of universalism, the belief that all will eventually be accepted by God. The form of universalism for which I would argue, semi-restorationism, says that though all will be reconciled to God and know the joy of knowing

Summary

God, those who have finally rejected God will lack the fullness of joy and completion possessed by those who have willingly chosen God and God's will for them. Prior to being accepted by God, they will also endure a limited time of punishment for their sins since they had rejected God's offer of forgiveness. Thus all people must make the decisions which will determine their final relationship with God.

All people must in this life, or in another very much like this one, be given a long enough lifetime and sufficient mental capacity to make the decisions which will determine their eternal destiny. The Recipient Oriented Theodicy says that such decisions must occur for all people within a context of varying degrees of suffering.

Christians who seek to defend their beliefs rarely appeal to this very biblical answer. How such fundamental biblical passages as Job 1 and 2 which establish this theodicy can be so overlooked, ignored, or misunderstood is sometimes difficult to understand. I would suggest that it is in Job 1 and 2 and similar portions of the Bible that the best answers will be found for the problem of human suffering. The church would do well to return the Observer Oriented Theodicy and, even more so, the Recipient Oriented Theodicy to central places in its theology and philosophy of religion.

It may now be interesting to see how the conclusions of this study would apply to common arguments from the Problem of Evil which are critical of God's existence. I will give just one example.

Stenger's Complaint

The late Victor Stenger did a little imagination game. He asked, What if I'm wrong about my atheism and someday stand before God at the judgment seat? He thought up a little speech to give God.[1] This is how it would sound:

"How dare you, God, to ask me to justify my life. You who created a world in which you impose great suffering on your creatures. You who created earthquakes and tsunamis to kill not terrorist or despots or child abusers but instead hundreds of thousands of the poorest, most underprivileged people in the world. You kill thousands of children every day from hunger. You refuse to relieve the suffering of the dying. You force animals to kill one another to survive.

---

1. Stenger, lecture.

PART I: HUMAN SUFFERING, THE GREATEST PROBLEM FOR BELIEF IN GOD

"You didn't have to do this God. With your unlimited power you could have made a universe with no pain or death. The universe you created is certainly big enough, vast enough. If you love humans so much, why did you confine us to this tiny planet and wait five billion years to make us? You could have made us so we could live anywhere, even in space.

"All of this was in your control God. You could have made a wonderful world for your creatures, but you didn't. So it is you, God, not I who have everything to answer for."

I think we can imagine God's response. Perhaps it might go something like this:

"Since your intelligence is so vast, Victor, you know that I could never have justification for what I have done. Strange, but I don't recall seeing you there when I created the universe and planned its laws. Human intelligence compared to mine is like a snail's intelligence compared to a human's, and yet you presume to know that my unfathomable purposes do not exist.

"You refuse to acknowledge that those who suffer may have any reason for their suffering. Like my servant Job, many face suffering because they need to be creatures who, in the face of pain, freely choose the good. They can only become the kind of creatures I desire them to be as they make those choices. I need to know if, in suffering, they will reject me or cling to me; if they will seek me, the one who yet deserves their commitment. When my purposes are fulfilled I will give them back much more for all they have endured. It will be to them as though they had never suffered pain. But I must do this after I have accomplished my purpose. My reason for allowing this pain must be fulfilled.

"Yes, I allow pain to children who do not deserve it. I could have prevented their suffering but I had reason for not preventing it. One reason is that I need to know if *you* will seek to stop their pain. Will you have compassion for them? Will you learn to have my heart, my anguish for their suffering? I want you to change but you cannot unless I put them before you to test you. When the testing is finished I will recompense their suffering. One day they will acknowledge that their suffering was not worth comparing to the joy they will then have. Yet you will not acknowledge that this could even be possible. You close your eyes to my purposes even when I make them known to you.

"Being so wise, you know that I should have created a world without suffering or death, as if my only reason for creating you was to give you an idyllic, endless life. You have never considered that my reasons may be to produce something more than mere creatures who endure a pointless and empty existence.

"With your great wisdom you know that I could never have good reason for allowing one animal to die. You rage against animal suffering and presume I have no reason for making this so. You do not even know how much they feel and yet you revile me for this? Shouldn't you suspect that I would have reasons you could never understand?

"I give you a world with plenty of room and you complain that I did not give you the vast spaces of the cosmos. Thousands of microbes live on the head of a pin with plenty of room for all; if they could think, would they complain if they knew how much space I had given you?

"I gave the earth to man and woman to tend and care for, to protect and value, but they have not controlled and limited their own populations and they have raped and devoured the earth. I gave them the intelligence to manage it, and what they could not know I would have shown them had they called upon me for wisdom. They wonder why their crops no longer grow, disease plagues their animals, and their oceans are depleted. They wonder why they must desert their land and cram themselves into urban squaller. Or seeking room they consume the lands of others and slaughter their inhabitants. They say they have no space and yet they have done this all to themselves.

"I have justified my acts to you up to all that your little mind could grasp. I created you with enough intelligence to understand that you have no good reason to accuse me of evil, yet you chose to reject that knowledge and wallow in your hatred. You would rather cling to your desired beliefs and your resentment no matter how self-destructive they are.

"I created you to know me. I created you incomplete until you let me fulfill all that is missing in you. Despite your hatred, I still long for you and desire your restoration. But for now I must let you have what you ask for, and all that you want is to be far from me.

"So yes, Victor, as I do for all of my children, I do for you: I do ask you to justify your life. Now I want to know what you have to say for yourself."

Part II

Bad Religion?

11

What Makes a Religion Bad?

DOES RELIGION PRODUCE MORE harm than good? Religions have been accused of producing or encouraging everything from psychological manipulation and unhappy lives to horrors as great as human sacrifice, inquisitions, pogroms, and witch burnings. This and the following chapters will evaluate such accusations and also question whether similar evils result from secular ideologies. After comparing nonreligious systems and conditions with religious ones, we will compare them with Christianity specifically.

I think the most basic and fundamental reasons for many of the evils just mentioned boil down to just a few factors. I also think that we will see that these factors are present in related secular beliefs and organizations just as much as religious ones. Of course the issue is more complicated than I let on. John Stackhouse comments about contemporary violence which is often blamed on religious commitment: "Sociologist David Martin (among many others) has demonstrated that religion is rarely the main cause of violence. Land, wealth, security, prestige, and vengeance are the perennial motives for war. Yet religion has frequently been deployed as a validation, fuel, and rewarder of violence on the grand scale."[1] I would like to point out some of the more crucial factors which tie into religion as well as secularism and which lead to greater social harm.

---

1. Stackhouse, "Who Are These 'People of Faith.' " See also Martin's *Does Christianity Cause War?*

Part II: Bad Religion?

Leaders

Any social group which adheres to or focuses on a belief or system of beliefs has some political content, some power over others. The more political power it possesses, the more it will attract evil people who want that power and the more it will tend to corrupt good people who have or seek power in that structure. Once evil people have power in a religious system, they will do evil to benefit themselves or that religion insofar as it benefits themselves.

This applies to people in all positions of power in all religions from Popes and Dali Lamas who raise armies to fight their enemies to local pastors who require submission and obedience of their congregations. But notice this same problem applies to secular systems as well. It applies to any organization that exercises power over its constituents or over outsiders. It afflicts governments, political parties, and businesses as easily as churches, mosques, and temples. Secular institutions possess political power and attract evil people who want that power but they also attract good people who can be corrupted by that power.

Commitment

A second reason for some of the evils we see manifest in religious organizations and institutions is the fact that they often engender such strong commitment to themselves. The more strongly you are committed to a belief system, the greater evils you will be willing to commit to defend or advance that system. You may be willing to kill or torture those who oppose you if you are committed and dedicated to your system strongly enough.

But again, this same problem applies to nonreligious systems. Just as deeply committed religious leaders or followers have killed heretics out of their commitment to their beliefs, so Marxist rebels or Nazi Brownshirts have killed out of their commitment to their ideology.

Of course there are still other factors which can lead to religious evils but they all follow from one's desire to benefit or advance oneself or any institution or ideology to which one is attached. Imagine that you are a peasant in nineteenth-century Russia. You may hate the Jews living in the village next to you because they look and dress and live differently than you do, and they do not want any social contact with you beyond what is economically necessary. So when a local priest thinks you should help burn their village because he says they killed your Lord, you are more than willing to join in and to accept that reason for doing so. Now if you know what your Lord taught, you may be more hesitant to do this. But if you want to hate and if you have leaders who push you on to greater hatred, then for you that may outweigh all that Jesus taught about loving your neighbor. As David Martin puts it, "You are right to be shocked by the Inquisition but you are not right to blame Galilee and the religion of love."[2]

Notice that in this example the religious nature of the evil, the persecution of one's Jewish neighbors by people who call themselves Christians, is only incidental to the evil. We have no good evidence that the same persecution would not occur in a completely secular setting with a completely nonreligious motivation. If the adjacent village is made up of immigrants and both the natives and the "foreigners" have no religion but they do have different dress, customs, language, etc., the same persecution will just as easily result. Hitler's anti-Semitism was largely a secular hatred, a hatred based on his perception of this different people group with its different culture and way of life whom he saw as harming his own self-identified people group and its way of life. In fact, we have no strong evidence of any religious influence on Hitler's anti-Semitism. His was a racial not a religious anti-Semitism.[3]

Ethical Foundations

Now there is one mitigating factor we have just alluded to which will affect these influences toward evil: the ethical content or foundation of a belief system. When we have a Marxist ideology that says it's okay to kill people to establish a Marxist regime, then Marxist followers have little problem killing anyone who hinders their progress. But suppose you are a deeply committed Catholic in the Middle Ages and your Pope tells you to kill his opponents. Because your core religion clearly tells you that it is wrong to kill under such conditions, you would face a moral conflict. No matter how much the Christian teaching is twisted to fit the desires of corrupt religious leaders, so long as one has access to those original teachings, one is still aware that they could never allow such a thing.

Religious leaders are sometimes able to override those original teachings but only by great effort and only as they secure sufficient power. Often

2. Martin, *Does Christianity Cause War*, 13.
3. Weikart, *Hitler's Religion*, 15–37, 147–71, 275–86.

Part II: Bad Religion?

such efforts to diminish the ethical content of the original founder's teachings end in protest or even protest movements within those religions. For example, the abuse of indulgences was a large factor leading to the Reformation. There were always monks like Berthold of Regensburg, the Franciscan who went around preaching that it is wrong to oppress the Jews. There were always some like the Jesuits who opposed the enslavement of the native Americans of Latin America. There have always been protest movements when religious authorities attempted to override the original ethical content of their religion.

Sometimes those leaders who wanted to modify or remove the original ethical teachings attempted to keep the people from those teachings. There is some evidence, for example, that in the last few centuries as Christians came to have more open access to the Bible than they had in previous centuries and so far as they accepted the authority of the Bible, anti-Semitism generally decreased.

The core ethical teachings of both secular and religious institutions and ideologies will have a great affect on how much evil will result. Those with evil ethical foundations will cause the greatest amount of evil (e.g., Hitler's National Socialism). Those with little or no ethical content will produce little evil and little good. Those belief systems with good ethical content will produce much good and will not as easily or quickly be overcome by corrupt leaders and evil movements within those systems. It took centuries for Christianity to become as corrupted as it eventually became when it claimed the right to take human lives or solicited or forced the state to do so to coerce religious beliefs. Those who have a very strong commitment to a belief system will be less likely to resort to violence to defend or advance it if that system teaches respecting others and their right to determine their beliefs. They will be even less likely to use force if their beliefs also promote love and care for others.

Just sticking a god or gods into a system of belief does not make it better or worse than it was before. The God has to be good and will judge all people as they deserve and, ideally, will motivate people to be good. Now if the god happens to be evil, a lot of evil may result. We can easily guess what will happen when a religion tells us the gods happen to like a lot of human sacrifices or self-torture or torture of others, for example. Sadly, there have been religions like that.

12

Are the Religious Worse than the Secular?

THE AZTECS MAY HAVE been the cruelest civilization in history. They're the only large scale society we know of to practice mass human sacrifice and cannibalism. Annual wars secured thousands of victims. According to Spanish accounts, a victim would have a rope tied around him and he would then be thrown into a kind of low burning fire pit until he was vomiting and covered with huge blisters. Then he was pulled out to have his heart torn out. The body was butchered, cooked, and eaten. Of course it wasn't only pre-Columbian Americans like the Incas, Aztecs, and Mayans who practiced human sacrifice. There have always been bad religions just as there have always been bad secular institutions and belief systems.[1]

If the accounts we have are accurate, the Aztec religion required thousands of human sacrifices each year whereas we know that the early Christian religion asked for people to love their enemies and care for the persecuted and outcasts. Can we avoid the conclusion that the first must certainly be categorized as evil, the latter as good? If we go on nothing more than this expressed ethical content, the teachings of Jesus and the Aztec mythology, this conclusion is almost impossible to deny.

Certainly someone may protest that in the Hebrew Bible, God commanded the Israelites to wipe out an entire population. Doesn't the biblical account give us reason to see the Christian and Aztec religions as very similar ethically? If Christianity worships the God who ordered this genocide, can it be seen as any less evil? We will look at the Canaanite conquest a little later in more detail. But until this problem can be dealt with, the Christian

---

1. Carroll and Shiflett, *Christianity on Trial*, 103–4.

Part II: Bad Religion?

God being either exonerated or condemned, it seems that the ethical teachings of Jesus and his high view of God's goodness and justice must for the time being hold the upper hand and with that we must hold Christianity as possibly the highest ethical religion we know of.

Physicist Steven Weinberg said that "with or without [religion], you would have good people doing good things and evil people doing evil things. But for good people to do evil things, that takes religion."[2] I think we should see that this is not true, at least if we are considering religions with good ethical foundations. Our discussion of the Milgram experiments later in this chapter points out how readily normal people can be made to do horrendous evil. The history of the Third Reich certainly illustrates this. Numerous examples can be given of normal nonreligious people who were enticed to do great evils because of social pressures within this evil regime and of religious people who resisted these pressures and paid with their lives. We will examine a couple of examples of the latter shortly.

Current sociological studies generally support the claim that religion does more good than harm. In a study written for the *Skeptical Inquirer*, analysts concluded that "the data consistently point to a negative association between religiosity and criminal behavior and a positive association between religiosity and prosocial behavior."[3] Though the writers were still willing to entertain the possibility that "the world would be 'better'—more humane—without religion" pending further evidence or analysis, the current evidence is more strongly against it. Laurence Iannoccone points out that modern social science confirms the "links between religiosity and a wide range of economically important social behavior, such as criminal activity, drug and alcohol consumption, physical and mental health, and marriage, fertility, and divorce."[4]

We should notice that these were generally studies which assumed the dominant religions of the Western world such as some form of Christianity. The ethical foundation of Christianity must be a primary factor producing this much good.

The negative evidence like historical instances of religious oppression (e.g., persecution of those who oppose or simply disregard accepted

---

2. Weinberg, address at the Conference on Cosmic Design; cited in a slightly altered form in Dawkins, *God Delusion*, 249. Weinberg has made essentially this same statement more than once.

3. Lilienfeld and Ammirati, "Better Off Without Religion?"

4. Iannoccone, "Economics of Religion," 1475.

religious beliefs and practices) can be explained without finding fault with religion per se. They can be explained by social and other factors such as those we have looked at, factors which are not intrinsically or uniquely religious: the ethical content of the religions considered, the degree of commitment of religious followers, the political power of the religious leaders. So even if the world were more dominated by bad religions (religions with bad ethical bases) or if good religions were given too much political power and became sufficiently controlled by evil leaders, we might not expect to find it to be worse than a world without religions. We cannot be sure that had we no bad religions that they wouldn't have been replaced by equally bad governments (e.g., Hitler's National Socialism, Stalin's Communism, etc.) or other oppressive secular organizations.

Certainly the witch hunts, the Inquisition, and the pograms would never have occurred had there been no Christianity. Yet because secular systems have produced evils quite comparable to these religious atrocities, we cannot be sure that secular atrocities and horrors would not have arisen to more than make up for what was lost. We need to remember that Pol Pot destroyed a quarter of Cambodia's population, about one and a half to two million murders; Stalin killed twenty million; Mao up to seventy million. If Mao's, Stalin's, and Pol Pot's regimes could pop up in such secular milieux or from such strongly atheistic philosophical backgrounds, how can we think the world would have had any less evil and oppression had the church never existed, especially after we have seen (and will see) how much good has come from Christianity?

Good people who follow a *good* religion can be corrupted to do evil, yes, but more often, good nonreligious people can be corrupted to do evil. Whenever we have those social forces which provide a strong temptation for good people to do evil, to resist those social forces one would more often need a strong moral foundation such as we find in the highly ethical religions.

The stronger one's commitment to a religion with strong ethical standards, the more likely one will resist the temptation to evil. It is almost paradoxical that this motivation to do good as we find it among those with a strong religious commitment is in tension with the increased temptation to protect that religion at any cost. The stronger the ethical foundation, the less likely will those adherents defend that religion by force.

History tells us that ostensive religious atrocities were rarely greater than those committed by the state. When heretics would be tortured under

Part II: Bad Religion?

the Inquisition, local kings and nobility would likewise torture peasants who did not pay their taxes in time or who committed other minor crimes. Secular governments would usually use torture much more extensively than did any of their corrupt religious counterparts.[5] People on trial in a secular court would often blaspheme simply so that they could be sent over to a religious court to be tried there instead.

I would challenge anyone to show me that any morally corrupt religion has produced more harm than any corresponding evil secular institutions. Even the Aztec mass human sacrifices hardly differed from Pol Pot's gruesome democide. In fact, if we were to compare nothing but sheer numbers looking at the quantity of people killed under clearly religious persecution compared to innocent people killed by secular institutions from the time of the Crusades, the proportion is about a hundred to one—one hundred people were killed by secular powers for each person killed under religious persecution and war.[6]

Now one observation might be in order once we recognize that zeal for a religious or secular system often results in violence to advance or defend that system. Might someone suggest that we should try to somehow rid ourselves of any human propensity to strong religious or secular commitment? We must ask ourselves, even if we could achieve a Brave New World, people with no strong commitment to anything, is that what we want? I believe that we have too much of a world of mindless masses already and it results in some of the most horrible human conditions we can imagine.

The first problem is that those who lack a strong commitment to a system or belief too easily give themselves to any available ideology, even those they have no good reason to embrace and which may be very harmful. People want something to commit themselves to, something to live for. Many will accept beliefs they would otherwise never seriously consider so long as this might fulfill their need to have something to which they can commitment themselves.

The second problem is that lack of commitment in our modern societies results in some of the most horrendous crimes we could ever witness; everything from the Frank murder by Leob and Leopold in the 1920s, the most famous of modern "thrill killings," to similar murder-for-fun crimes today. No, the answer is *definitely not* that we should make sure people have no strong commitments to anything. The answer is that we should first

---

5. Carroll and Shiflett, *Christianity on Trial*, 105.
6. D'Souza, *What's So Great About Christianity?* 219.

consider secular and religious belief systems which offer good evidence for their claims and then evaluate the good or evil which may follow from those systems. We need to accept, even commit ourselves to, the system which is backed by the better evidence no matter how much harm we think it may produce. Of course, we will only benefit if the better evidenced system does produce more good than harm.

Consider the nature of the church which gave rise to the Inquisition. It was a slow and somewhat gradual process. But it was only after the Catholic Church came under the control of evil leaders that the ethical content of the New Testament teaching could be so abrogated that such an abomination could be accepted. The teaching of the New Testament is clear that one cannot do what these people did. To so contradict the full ethical teachings of Jesus and the New Testament, one simply cannot be called a Christian without making the word meaningless. When Jesus taught that you should love your enemies and do good to those who hate you, his words *cannot* be twisted to mean you can burn them at the stake.

I am not singling out on the Catholic Church. Similar atrocities happened in the Protestant and Eastern churches as well. Witness how Calvin advocated and had part in the execution of Servetus. In the New Testament times the worst the church could do to apostates, heretics, or members living in unrepentant sin was to exclude them from the church. And then they were to be received back with love and full acceptance if they repented (1 Cor 5:1–2, 4, 11–13; 2 Cor 2:6–11). That the church could become so corrupted within just a few short centuries must primarily be explained by the influences we have mentioned: evil leaders who allowed only their own corrupt teachings to be heard or accepted, zealous followers who disregarded Jesus' words so that they could defend their religion by force, and others in the church who embraced the new teachings when it fit their own desires.

Do Evil Leaders Make Evil Religions?

So far we have been discussing the question of whether in principle religions generally produce more good or evil than secular organizations or ideologies. Before looking at specific examples we should also think about whether a religion should be considered evil simply because of the evil we see committed by its members without that religion's authorization.

Part II: Bad Religion?

History is filled with accounts of religious leaders enacting pogroms and inquisitions or even lesser crimes of oppression and psychological manipulation. We are aware of the scandals popularized in the press of people like Jim Bakker, Jimmy Swaggart, and the pedophile Catholic priests. There is just no way to completely remove evil people from different religions though some religions are better at doing so than others. If some religions do not at least seek to glean out their corrupt leaders, it is here that we can begin to judge the entire religion as evil. Let me give an example that involves a very different religion from those the press will usually focus on. This will help us to see that this problem applies to all religions, even those which purport to be very benevolent.[7]

The late Chögyam Trungpa was the leader of the Tibetan Buddhist organization, Vajradhatu, in Boulder, Colorado from 1973 to 1986. He was previously the head of a monastery in Tibet before the Chinese Communist take over. In Boulder, some members, besides having to pay normal yearly dues, were sometimes also solicited to work as unpaid maids and butlers at his mansion. Some female followers testify that he solicited them to sleep with him and were accused of arrogance if they refused. It is considered arrogant to question a leader of Trungpa's status since your "perceptions are not clear until you are enlightened," as he supposedly was. He reassured them that they would someday perceive the value of the experience. One woman who gave in to his advances spoke of being psychologically overwhelmed and of the pressure to obey. Some ex-members claim that all of one's critical faculties are surrendered to the Rinpoche, that one loses one's ability to question.

Trungpa also had a problem with drinking and would sometimes give his lectures obviously drunk. Some of his apologists said he just did this to show people how they look. There is good reason to believe that his death in 1987 was related to his alcoholism.

And then there was an incident that is now referred to as "The Party." In 1975 at a retreat at Snowmass, Colorado, a couple, poet W. S. Merwin and his girlfriend, Dana Naone, had earned Trungpa's displeasure for their "aloofness," for keeping to themselves for all but the essential times of meditation, lecture, and ritual. They probably did this because of the rumors of orgy-like parties common on the campus, some of which they may have

---

7. More details or discussion concerning the following events can be found in the following: Marin, *Harper's*, February 1979, 51–58; Gaeddert, *Rocky Mountain News*, 14 July 1980, 4; 15 July 1980, 8.

even witnessed. Trungpa was irritated that they left a halloween party early and sent for them. They refused to come and he sent his guards to force them to come. Standing before him and the people at the party, Trungpa made a derogatory comment about the woman's race, she was Chinese, and asked her what she was doing with a white man. He ordered them stripped and the woman screamed for someone to call the police. One man tried to intervene only to be overpowered by the guards. One account has it that another man tried to stop them, was struck by Trungpa, and was carried away. Obviously the guards could not have stopped them had even a few more among this mass of people attempted to intervene. And one has to wonder how the guards could be so brainwashed as to be so readily willing to carry out a criminal act.

One is reminded of the Milgram experiments in the 1960s, psycho-social experiments testing just how willingly normal people will obey an authority figure.[8] Under the guise of a different experiment, subjects were asked to give increasingly larger electric shocks to unseen participants when they gave wrong responses to given questions. They could hear the victim's cries and pleas, increasing as the voltage increased. The victims were not actually shocked but acted as though they were. In the first set of experiments an unexpectedly large proportion of the subjects, twenty-six out of forty (65 percent), gave what they believed to be potentially lethal shocks, the highest voltage marked on the dial, to the actors. They did so simply because they were told to do so by those leading the experiment, people in "white lab jackets." Some have argued that some of the subjects may have believed the experiment was a ruse and believed that no shocks were actually being administered. It may even be that as few as half of the number of those who turned the dial to maximum voltage (33 percent of the participants) believed they were actually giving lethal shocks. But this is still a very troubling number.

The experiment showed that people will uncritically obey authority figures, in this case not religious authorities, to the very great harm of others. The experiment has been repeated only to reveal similar or even higher percentages of potential executioners. We should also notice that women were no less likely to administer lethal dosages than men. Moving from the experimental to the historical, Clay Jones has demonstrated merely from historical events of the last century that it was just normal people like you

---

8. Milgram, "Behavioral Study of Obedience," 371–78.

Part II: Bad Religion?

and I, not a very few morally depraved monsters and psychopaths, who had carried out some of the most horrible atrocities in history.[9]

Leaders in virtually any religion have oppressed others in similar and even worse ways than Trungpa had. The question then is, If a religious leader will do this, does that make the religion they lead or profess evil? No. Sometimes they act in contradiction to their religion's teachings. Only the individual who has committed this wrong should be judged. A religion can only be judged as evil if it can be shown that its beliefs are evil or that it somehow promotes harm. If Trungpa is still honored today as a great religious leader in Tibetan Buddhism, unless he had repented of what he had done, then that religion is morally deficient. As much as we may be angry at, say, the Catholic Church for attempting to cover up the acts of child molestation by pedophile priests, at least the church admits that these acts are wrong.

The priests who did this and those who tried to cover it up should be prosecuted but the Catholic Church as a whole should not be held accountable. If the Catholic Church should be held accountable, then shouldn't Penn State University also be held accountable because Coach Sandusky molested children? Blame the individuals responsible not the organization they work under, unless that organization as a whole endorses their action. If the guilty priests give us reason to reject the Catholic Church as a totally wicked institution, shouldn't all universities and colleges, all day-care centers and elementary schools, be judged the same? Should the former be vilified but not the latter?

---

9. Jones, *Why Does God Allow Evil?* chap. 2.

13

What Good Comes from Christianity?

Christianity's Motivation for Good

How does Christianity stand as to the good or evil we should expect it would produce? We will need to look at some examples shortly. Is it different from theistic religions generally? Those who accept Christianity believe that there is a life after death in which justice will be finally carried out and those who follow and obey Christ and live moral lives will be rewarded and honored in God's sight. If we are merely considering a generic form of theism, it may be doubted how certainly God will carry out justice in the next life. In Christianity this is not doubted. The Christian who believes justice will be done is more likely to do good when tempted to do evil than the atheist or generic theist who believes justice will not be done or has no reason to think it will be done in the next life.

Christianity says the death of Jesus showed how much God did to bring us reconciliation with God. It says this is the only way we can be brought back to God. Our free choice to sin, to harm others or ourselves, separates us from a perfect and good God who can have nothing to do with sin. Jesus said that to know God is eternal life (John 17:3). It is our greatest joy, our greatest good. It is our greatest harm and loss to be separated from God. Because God is absolutely good and absolute love, we were created because God wanted there to be more who would know this good, this greatest of all joys. Greater good occurs as more people relate to and know and love God. The Christian believes God willingly endured pain to an extreme only God could endure. For God to endure this to bring us reconciliation shows how much God loves us. This brings us strong motivation to love and obey God.

Jesus taught that his followers are not only to obey and accept his moral and spiritual teachings but they are to take up their cross, to be willing to suffer and die for him. And believing in God's sacrifice, they have a strong motivation to do so. So Christianity, or at least a strongly biblical Christianity, requires a very strong commitment to God and to Jesus and it provides a strong motivation to obey Jesus' commands. As such, Christianity also provides a strong motivation for good since all of Jesus' commands can arguably be claimed to produce more good than harm. Also Jesus commanded his followers to simply do good to others; thus we are to do the good we know to do by nature. Later we will look at some commands which some will claim have produced harm. Until then we should assume that most of his teachings produce more good than harm and that very possibly they all do.

Christianity's ethical content is not surpassed by any other religion. Confucius said to not do unto others as you would not have done unto yourself. Jesus' statement, "Do to others as you would have them do to you" (Luke 6:31), thus represents an advance, though at this point they are both very close. This and similar teachings by Jesus like, "Love your neighbor as yourself" (Matt 19:19), if consistently and universally followed would rid the world of racism, slavery, sexism, classism. The problem is not with New Testament teachings, it is with our failure to follow it.

We can hardly find a higher testimony to the good Christianity provides than from some of Hitler's statements. According to Albert Speer, Hitler said something like the following more than once: "You see, it's been our misfortune to have the wrong religion. Why didn't we have the religion of the Japanese, who regard sacrifice for the Fatherland as the highest good? The Mohammedan religion too would have been much more compatible to us than Christianity. Why did it have to be Christianity with its meekness and flabbiness?"[1] Hitler wanted a cruel, unforgiving race and nation, an amoral psychopathic hardness and dedication completely obedient to him alone. Yet as much as he hated and derided Christianity, it was Christians who were constantly refusing to follow his laws, who were hiding Jewish families—these were the ones who resisted Hitler as much or more than any other group.

---

1. Speer, *Inside the Third Reich*, 96.

What Good Comes from Christianity?

And Speer's statement is not a contested quotation. Unlike so many Hitler quotations we run into, especially on the internet, this one was given by a close friend who had no reason to misrepresent what he said. Also, this quotation was not given in any of Hitler's propaganda speeches or for propaganda purposes. This agrees with Goebbels's statement in his diary; he said of Hitler that he was "deeply religious but entirely anti-Christian."[2]

At this point let me give just a few examples of the good that has come from Christianity specifically, at least from those Christians who have taken the New Testament seriously and sought to follow its teachings consistently.

The American Irish and the Catholic Church

The first example we will consider might be titled, How the Catholic Church saved the Irish in America.[3] In the 1840s and 50s, with the great potato blight in Ireland and with England's political and moral indifference to the poverty and mass starvation, the Irish emigrated to America in the hundreds of thousands. Especially in the large cities like New York and Boston, the uneducated and skill-less new Irish immigrants faced cultural and economic shock and despair. Drunkenness, addiction to opium and laudanum, prostitution, and illegitimacy were epidemic. Children were abandoned by the thousands. Murderous gangs roamed the streets. The death rate was staggering.

Priests and nuns were virtually the only ones willing to work for social reform among the Irish. In New York, Bishop John Hughes began by founding numerous churches and schools in Irish neighborhoods; he recruited priests and nuns to preach self-help, sexual purity, temperance, and mutual aid. The St. Vincent de Paul Society was brought in to financially aid the impoverished, requiring work for aid whenever possible. Societies formed to get children off the streets. Nuns placed domestics in the homes of the wealthy. The Irish Emigrant Society was created functioning as an employment agency.

The Irish, who were originally seen as a criminal class, within thirty to forty years made up the the pillars of the criminal justice system. Three quarters of the police were Irish. The Irish proportion of arrests for violent crimes dropped from 50 percent to 10 percent. Irish parts of the city became known for their peacefulness, order, and cleanliness; in mid-century they

---

2. Goebbels, diary entry 29 December 1939, 250; cited in Weikart, *Hitler's Religion*, 2.
3. Carrol and Shiflet, *Christianity on Trial*, 201–4.

were known for their filth, violence, and disease. Family life became strong and nourishing. Alcoholism and drug addiction withered away. Children entered professions like the priesthood, politics, commerce, entertainment, and professional sports. Since then Catholics in America have built numerous aid societies, homes for the aged and infirm, hospitals (six hundred today), and orphanages.

We talked earlier about Weinberg's statement that good people will do good things and bad people will do bad things, "but for good people to do evil things, that takes religion." I think we have seen that more often the opposite is true, at least if we are talking about religions to which their adherents are deeply committed and which have strong moral content. It takes a highly motivating religion with a high ethical content like Christianity to get bad people to become good people. It is much less common to find a nonreligious system that will get bad people to so change.

Father Kolbe

My second example shows the very powerful motivating force Christianity has for bringing its followers to do extraordinary morally courageous acts. Chuck Colson recounts the story of Father Kolbe in his book, *The Body*.[4]

Hitler was in power and had conquered Poland, but he hated the Poles and wanted to make them a slave race. Poland became his proving grounds to begin mass extermination of Christians. In West Prussia alone two-thirds of the parish priests were arrested while the rest fled to escape. A third of those arrested were killed in the first month. Only three in a hundred were in their parishes by 1941. Murdered Polish priests numbered in the thousands.[5] In Germany priests and pastors were sent to death camps for such crimes as "preaching love of neighbor, for insisting Jesus was a Jew, for warning S.S. men that they could not abjure their faith to achieve promotion, for offering requiem Masses even for relatives of Communists."[6]

Father Kolbe was a Franciscan monk in Poland. As a child he had a dream. In the dream God asked him to choose between a white crown of purity or a red one of martyrdom. He chose both. As an adult he prayed for the world and his friary produced literature to spread the Christian

---

4. Colson, *The Body*, 318–26.
5. Carrol and Shiflet, *Christianity on Trial*, 118.
6. O'Malley, "The Priests of Dachau," 352; cited in Carrol and Shiflet, *Christianity on Trial*, 128.

message. After the Nazi's took Poland he was arrested for publishing unauthorized literature and taken to Auschwitz. He ministered to fellow prisoners, hearing their confessions, praying with them, comforting them. Under its torturous work conditions and near starvation rations he once collapsed, was beaten, and left for dead. He miraculously survived.

When a prisoner escaped, ten other prisoners would be painfully executed in retaliation. One night a prisoner escaped from Kolbe's barracks and ten men were selected for execution. At roll call as they began to be led away one of the men cried out, "My poor wife, my poor children, what will they do?" Before they were taken to the starvation bunker, Kolbe broke ranks and ran to the commandant. Normally the guards would simply shoot anyone daring to break ranks, let alone anyone who would dare to speak to a German officer. Instead the commandant screamed out, "Halt, what does this Polish pig want of me?" Kolbe asked to take the place of one of the ten men, the one who was so distraught about his family. He persuaded the commandant by pointing out how worn and old and weak he was. The other prisoner was stronger and of more use to them alive. Colson writes, "For the first and last time, the commandant looked Kolbe in the eye. 'Who are you?' he asked. . . . 'I am a Catholic priest,'" Kolbe answered.[7]

In the starvation bunker, denied both food and water, the naked prisoners would drink their own urine. "Past prisoners had spent their dying days howling, attacking one another, clawing the walls in a frenzy of despair. But now, coming from the death box those outside heard the faint sounds of singing."[8] Kolbe was the last of the ten to die.

Lee and Leslie Strobel

My third example. Lee Strobel has interviewed a number of leading evangelical Christian scholars to bring together the best arguments for Christianity and the best responses to criticism. Some of his most popular books are, *The Case for Christ*, *The Case for Faith*, *The Case for the Real Jesus*, and *The Case for a Creator*. In one of his latest books, *The Case for Grace*, he tells a little more about his own story than we will cover here and he also interviews people from very different backgrounds, one of whom I will mention later. Like Lee and Leslie Strobel, the individuals we will look at now, their

---

7. Colson, *The Body*, 325.
8. Ibid., 325–26.

PART II: BAD RELIGION?

lives show how Christianity has enormously benefited themselves and others around them.

Strobel tells in the following account how as a hard-nosed journalist for the legal section of the *Chicago Tribune* and following his wife's acceptance of Christianity, he began investigating the evidence for himself. He eventually was persuaded and came to belief. But there was something in his account that caught my attention that he does not always bring up. His story exemplifies the valuable moral changes which occur in the lives of many who leave atheism to become Christians. Certainly there may be atheists who can boast of having moral standards and ideals which are just as good as those Strobel acquired, but the fact that these changes occurred after leaving his atheism gives reason to think that Christianity offers an improvement for many, probably most atheists who embrace Christianity. A popular movie has come out, *The Case for Christ*, which also portrays much of his story, but here is his account in his own words:

> [As an atheist] my number one value was to bring maximal pleasure into my life. It was to keep myself happy at all costs. So I lived a very immoral and profane and drunken and narcissistic and self-absorbed life—self-destructive in many ways. I had a lot of anger inside of me, a lot or rage inside of me. I think it was because I was always after that perfect high. I was always after that ultimate experience of pleasure and in the end nothing lived up to the hype. Everything let me down. Nothing was as good as it was advertised. So I was often in a rage.
>
> I remember once my wife and I got into an argument and my daughter was there. And I just blew up. And I remember I reared back and, boom, I kicked a hole right in our living room wall. And my wife's crying and our baby's crying.
>
> I'm going to tell you the ugliest thing about me. My little daughter, Allison, was just a toddler. If she was alone in the living room playing with some blocks, or train, or toys, or whatever, and she would hear me come home from work through the front door, her natural reaction was just to gather her toys and go in her room and close the door. "You gonna be drunk again? Hear me yelling and screaming and kicking holes in the wall? You know what, at least it's nice and quiet in here." Friends, that is the ugliest I could be.
>
> My wife was agnostic. And so one day we moved into a condominium building outside Chicago and the woman downstairs was a Christian. And this woman, Linda, became best friends with my wife Leslie. And it was very natural in her friendship for this

woman to talk about Jesus with Leslie. And Leslie wasn't hostile to this stuff; nobody had ever told her this stuff before. So she asked questions. They talked about God. They talked about the Bible. Leslie went to church with her. And finally after many months after checking these things out, Leslie came up to me one day and said, "Lee, I made a big decision." I said, "What?" She said, "I've decided to become a follower of Jesus Christ."

And I thought, "Oh no." This was the worst possible news that I could get. Honestly, the first word that went through my mind: "divorce." "I don't need this stuff. This is bait and switch. I married one Leslie, now she's gonna be some holy roller or something. I didn't sign up for this stuff." I was just gonna walk out.

I'll tell you how mature I was. She had a very beautiful garden she would carefully tend. . . . I went out and mowed the lawn, and I just mowed down her flower bed.

And what surprised me—I stuck around for a while—what surprised me were the positive things that started to change in her character and her values and the way she related to me and the children. It was winsome, it was attractive. So finally one Sunday morning I was sleeping off a hangover and Leslie's getting ready to go to church. She said, "Lee, why don't you come to church with me today?" And I thought, "You know what, I'm gonna go." Find out about this cult that she's involved in.

So I went with her to a church. . . . And the pastor gets up to preach. . . . And he gave a talk called basic Christianity. . . . And all my misconceptions and objections about the Christian faith were just getting knocked down one after the other. And I remember walking out that day saying two things: number one, I was still an atheist. He did not convince me that day that God exists. But number two, I realized, you know what? if this stuff is true, this has huge implications for my life. So what I decided to do was take my legal training and my journalism training and systematically investigate. Is there any credibility to Christianity or any other world religion? And this launched me onto what turned out to be a nearly two year investigation of the evidence.

During this time Leslie and a Christian friend had prayed together that God would change Lee's heart from stone to flesh. There is a passage in the Hebrew scripture in which God says, "I will remove from them their heart of stone and give them a heart of flesh" (Ezek 11:19). After his investigation, Lee came to believe and to commit his life to God through Jesus. He says the following:

Starting on that Sunday afternoon, now that I was a child of God, now that I could read the Bible with a new understanding, now that I became part of a church that was teaching the Bible and I could meet other Christians and learn to fellowship with them and I could learn to pray, . . . God began to answer their prayer [the prayer that God would change his heart from stone to flesh]. Because my values changed, and my character changed, and my morality changed, and my world view and my attitudes, and my relationships, and my priorities, . . . all these things overturned. So much so that my daughter Allison—this is a little girl who the first five years of her life only knew a dad who was absent or angry, kicking holes through walls, coming home drunk; that was her entire experience her first five years of her life. But starting on that Sunday afternoon, you know what she started to do? She started listening and she started to watch and she started to observe. Because her daddy was walking on a new path. Something was different. His priorities were changing. His attitudes were changing. He was changing in front of her eyes. . . . So finally five or six months later, it was a Sunday morning, she went up to her first year Sunday School teacher and then she went up to my wife Leslie, and you know what she said to her? "I want God to do for me what he's done for daddy."[9]

Just as Lee saw moral changes in his wife, now his daughter could see changes in him.

The ten Boom Family

The fourth example I want to bring up, the Dutch ten Boom family, is much like that of my earlier example of Father Kolbe at Auschwitz. This shows the very powerful motivating force Christianity has for bringing its followers to do extraordinary morally courageous acts. The following is taken from Corrie ten Boom's books *The Hiding Place* and *Father ten Boom*.

Isaac de Costa was a Portuguese Jew who became a prominent lawyer in Holland in the nineteenth century. He became a follower of Jesus and then began calling upon the churches to pray for the Jewish people. Deeply moved by his words, Willem ten Boom started a prayer group for this purpose in his home. His son, Casper, told of how "love for the Jews was spoon-fed to me from my very youngest years." One of Casper's daughters,

---

9. Strobel, from a talk given 12 March 2011.

Corrie, in turn relates that "as a result, deep respect and love for the Jews became a part of our home life."[10]

Casper sold and repaired watches and had business dealings with several Jewish wholesalers. Corrie, while only a child, would take the train with him on his business trips. Speaking of his visits with these Jewish businessmen, she says that "these were the visits we both liked best."

> After the briefest discussion of business, Father would draw a small Bible from his traveling case; the wholesaler, whose beard would be even longer and fuller than Father's, would snatch a book or scroll out of a drawer, clap a prayer cap onto his head; and the two would be off, arguing, comparing, interrupting, contradicting, reveling in each other's company.
>
> And then, just when I had decided that this time I had really been forgotten, the wholesaler would look up, catch sight of me as though for the first time, and strike his forehead with the heel of his hand.
>
> "A guest! A guest in my gate and I have offered her no refreshment!" And springing up he would rummage under shelves and into cupboards and before long I would be holding on my lap a plate of the most delicious treats in the world.[11]

This was not an intrusion into another person's privacy as some would caricature it. This is the kind of exchange of which the deepest friendships are made. To so sterilize relationships so that topics such as these should never be spoken is to strip friendships of any depth, openness, or honesty.

A Jewish watchseller owned a shop on the same street as Casper ten Boom. Mr. Kann consistently undersold and outsold the ten Boom shop. Once while walking with his grandson, Peter, the child pointed out Mr. Kann's shop and asked his grandfather if Mr. Kann were his competitor. "No," the old man replied, "he is my colleague. And do not forget," he continued, "he belongs to God's chosen people."[12]

During the Nazi occupation of Holland the ten Boom shop became something of a center for resistance work. A Jewish mother with her baby were sent there to find hiding. Corrie thought she had the perfect home when a local pastor brought a watch in for repair. His secluded house was set back in a large wooded park. At last she asked him,

---

10. ten Boom, *Father ten Boom*, 33.
11. ten Boom, *Hiding Place*, 25.
12. ten Boom, *Father ten Boom*, 146.

Part II: Bad Religion?

> "Would you be willing to take a Jewish mother and her baby into your home? They will almost certainly be arrested otherwise."
>
> Color drained from the man's face. He took a step back from me. "Miss ten Boom! I do hope you're not involved with any of this illegal concealment and undercover business. It's just not safe! Think of your father! And your sister—she's never been strong! . . ."
>
> . . . I pulled the coverlet from the baby's face.
>
> There was a long silence. The man bent forward, his hand in spite of himself reaching for the tiny fist curled round the blanket. For a moment I saw compassion and fear struggle in his face. Then he straightened. "No. Definitely not. We could lose our lives for that Jewish child!"
>
> Unseen by either of us, Father had appeared in the doorway. "Give the child to me Corrie," he said.
>
> Father held the baby close, his white beard brushing its cheek, looking into the little face with eyes as blue and innocent as the baby's own. At last he looked up at the pastor. "You say we could lose our lives for this child. I would consider that the greatest honor that could come to my family."
>
> The pastor turned sharply on his heels and walked out of the room.[13]

It wasn't long until Father ten Boom was granted this honor. Captured by the Gestapo, the entire household waited to be interrogated.

> Suddenly the chief interrogator's eye fell on Father. "That old man!" he cried. "Did he have to be arrested? You, old man!"
>
> Willem [Casper's son] led Father up to the desk. The Gestapo chief leaned forward. "I'd like to send you home, old fellow!" he said. "I'll take your word that you won't cause any more trouble."
>
> I could not see Father's face, only the erect carriage of his shoulders and the halo of white hair above them. But I heard his voice.
>
> "If I go home today," he said evenly and clearly, "tomorrow I will open my door again to any man in need who knocks."
>
> The amiability drained from the other man's face. "Get back in line!" he shouted. "*Schnell!* This court will tolerate no more delays!"[14]

---

13. ten Boom, *Hiding Place*, 99.
14. Ibid., 137–38.

Casper died within ten days. Two of his daughters were sent to Ravenbruk; one of them would die there. Others of his children and grandchildren would die in other concentration camps or as a result of their internment.

In 1844 Willem ten Boom opened his home to people who would pray for and identify with the Jewish people. One hundred years later their prayers were answered when Willem's son, grandchildren, and great-grandchildren came to fully identify with the Jewish people through imprisonment, torture, and death.

New Testament Moral Demands

A life like that of Casper ten Boom is the inevitable result of seeking to live consistently and uncompromisingly according to New Testament teachings. Jesus made it clear that the greatest commandment, next to that of loving God, is to love our neighbor as our very selves. And he also made it clear that everyone, and especially the most despised and rejected, is our neighbor (Luke 10:25–37) and that what we do to that person we do to him (Matt 25:40). Furthermore, we find in these writings a special honor and love accorded to the Jewish people. Even those Jewish opponents who were said to be "enemies" of all that Jesus and his followers taught were spoken of as specially "beloved for the sake of the fathers" (Rom 11:28 NKJV).

The problem is not with Christian scripture but rather with our ignoring or twisting its clear teaching. Like the pastor who refused to shelter the Jewish mother and her baby, his desire to protect his own life cost them theirs. Yet Jesus said that only those who are willing to lose their lives would gain life (Matt 16:25). It's incredible that one whose life profession is dedicated to proclaiming and admonishing others to follow Jesus' teaching can so completely ignore the message once it becomes uncomfortable.

Looking a little more closely at a point raised earlier, it is even more sobering to remember that Jesus said that what we do to the very least, the person of absolutely lowest esteem, the leper, the untouchable; what we've done to that person, we've done to him. And God's judgment upon us will depend upon what we have done to that person. Indeed, what we do "to the least of these," as Jesus said (Matt 25:31–46), will be enough to determine one's loss and separation from God in the age to come. This is the case even if we have trusted in Jesus for salvation; this is so whether we have otherwise lived the holiest life a person could imaginably live. And what again were these sins that Jesus considered of such enormous magnitude? Failure to comfort or aid the sick, the imprisoned, the oppressed; failure to feed the hungry or clothe the naked.

Christians Cannot Oppress Others

Jesus taught his followers that they cannot use force to defend him or his teachings. There is no place for oppressing others. To one who tried to defend him from capture he said that those who use the sword will die by it (Matt 26:51–52). To the Roman governor who condemned him to death, he said his servants could not fight because his kingdom is not of this world (John 18:36). He rebuked followers who wanted to call down fire from heaven on those who rejected him. Some texts, though less reliable, say that he told these disciples they do not know what spirit they are of and that he came not to destroy but to save (Luke 9:52–56). This is the one who taught us to do unto others as we would have done to ourselves (Matt 7:12) and to love and pray for our enemies and oppressors (5:44–47). Oppression cannot possibly follow from such teachings as these which were so foundational to his thought.

Too many people, even too many followers of Jesus, are unaware of how radical his way is. Too many have simply ignored his words. He told us that we need to take up our cross and follow him. The cross was a means of torturous execution. It meant that we should not expect anything less than pain and death. He told us that if we deny him before people, he will deny us before God. And he told us that what we've done to the least, we've done to him. So the pastor who denied this Jewish baby had denied Jesus, the one he claimed to hold as Lord and master. He was not willing to face death as Jesus had commanded him.

Christianity's Power to Motivate Moral Dedication

Followers of Jesus who will honestly hear his words feel a strongly motivating power in his death. They hold that because he gave so much to bring us back to God, indeed, because God gave so much in sending the Messiah for this purpose, the only appropriate response is one of grateful submission, commitment, and obedience to God and Messiah. Seeing how much God loved us, how much God gave for us, we fall in awed adoration and obedience.

The New Testament writings even go further than this: Looking at those who are the most dejected, the most unwanted, the most undesirable; we understand that God willingly became a man and endured the most excruciatingly painful death out of love for even one of these. So much God loved this one that we would think so little of. (Even a very minimalist Christian view omitting Jesus' deity would maintain that all that Jesus endured, all that he gave up, God also endured and sacrificed because God loved us so much.) How can we dare to look down upon this one God so values? God values him or her so much that Jesus said that what we do to this outcast, this untouchable, we do to him. We come to feel what God feels for this person. God's sacrifice for us motivates us to self-sacrifice. It's difficult to imagine any other religious belief, not to mention secular belief, having quite the same motivating power.

Peter Claver and Elizabeth of Hungary

Just a couple of more examples in passing. The seventeenth-century Jesuit, Peter Claver, spent his life nursing Africans caught in the slave trade. He would give a stricken black man his bed and sleep on the floor. Dorothy Day recounts that once when those "he had induced to help him ran from the room, panic-stricken before the disgusting sight of some sickness, he was astonished. 'You mustn't go,' he said, and you can still hear his surprise that anyone could forget such a truth: 'You mustn't leave him—it is Christ.'" The thirteenth-century Elizabeth of Hungary spent her life under the same compulsion. She once put in her bed a man stricken with leprosy "and later, going to tend him, saw no longer the leper's stricken face, but the face of Christ."[15]

Hang Pin

I mentioned earlier that I would take another example from Lee Strobel's book *The Case for Grace*.[16] This is the story of a Cambodian man called comrade Duch (pronounced *Doik*). He at one time also went by the name Hang Pin. This is shortened from Strobel's very moving account. When Pol Pot led the Khmer Rouge and took over Cambodia he wiped out about a

---

15. Ellsberg, *By Little and By Little*, 95.
16. Strobel, *Case for Grace*, 89–105, chap. 5.

Part II: Bad Religion?

quarter of the population, one and a half to two million people. Comrade Duch was in command of one particular interrogation center, S-21. Of the fourteen thousand who entered S-21, seven survived. It was Duch who ordered their torture and executions. When Viet Nam invaded Cambodia in 1979 and overthrew the Khmer Rouge, Duch fled but left detailed records of the torture and killing at S-21. He was tracked down, possibly by former Khmer Rouge soldiers for leaving this incriminating evidence. He and his wife were bayonetted and left for dead. His wife died but he survived.

Duch now went by the name Hang Pin. Pin, dealing with heavy depression and guilt, attended some Christian meetings he had heard about hoping this might help him. At one of the meetings he expressed the desire to ask for God's forgiveness and to commit his life to Christ. He told the person praying with him that he had done some very bad things and that he didn't think the families he had hurt could forgive him. The prayer counselor had lost a cousin in S-21. He did not ask about Pin's past, he only wanted to be sure that he was serious and repentant. He said Pin said he was sorry and appeared to be remorseful. He told Pin God loves him and can forgive him and then he prayed with him. The next day the usually depressed and dejected Pin was now excited and anxious to learn about this God who forgives. His life transformed, he started a church in his village. With military disruptions in his area he aided in refugee work and later worked with Christian organizations to provide medical and health care. Those he worked with and aided spoke of his dedication and care for them and their needs. He was greatly loved by those he helped.

Later a journalist tracked down the notorious Duch and questioned him. At first he was evasive but then he admitted everything. Even the journalist admitted that he genuinely appeared to be remorseful. "The Holy Spirit convicted my heart," Duch said, "I have to tell the world what I've done to my people."[17] Expecting his arrest, he said, "It's okay, they have my body, Jesus has my soul."[18] He said, "The first half of my life I thought God was very bad, that only bad people prayed to God. My fault is that I didn't serve God, I served men. I served Communism. I feel very sorry about the killings and the past—I wanted to be a good Communist." He said he had a new goal now. "I want to tell everyone about the gospel."[19]

17. Ibid., 101.
18. Ibid., 100.
19. Ibid., 99.

What Good Comes from Christianity?

Pin was tried and confessed his crimes and he said he would testify against other Khmer Rouge officials. At one time in his trial, at his request he was taken to S-21 with the few survivors who could be found and the families of those killed there. In tears he collapsed on the ground and apologized to them and asked for their forgiveness. He said he knew they could not forgive him but asked for them to give him the hope that someday they might. One survivor said, "Here are the words that I have longed to hear for thirty years."[20] Pin is now serving a lifetime prison sentence in Phnom Penh.

He made one final statement we may need to come back to later: "If I had Jesus before," he said, "I never would have done what I did. I never knew about his love."[21] We cannot find a more telling statement demonstrating the power of Christian belief and transformation to prevent horrendous evil.

I first gave two examples, the ten Booms and Father Kolbe in the concentration camps. These were examples of moral courage and sacrifice that an atheist would be far less likely to be willing to measure up to. In passing, I mentioned a couple of others who lived their lives as servants to the lowest social outcasts, to the most oppressed, because they believed that what they did they were doing for Jesus. We looked at an example of a moral change for the better in the lives of two people, Lee and Leslie Strobel. I mentioned a religious movement that produced moral changes that greatly affected our society, the changes in nineteenth-century Irish American society driven by agents of the Catholic Church. I mentioned finally commander Duch, a man responsible for the torture and murder of fourteen thousand people. Had he believed in Jesus at the time, he would never have committed such atrocities. I could go on with many more examples but I only wanted to give a diverse sampling to show some of the different kinds of moral good that come from Christianity.

How Did Christianity Survive?

The persecutions during the church's first centuries wiped out many Christians and provided such strong motivation for inquirers not to even consider the new sect that it is difficult to understand how the church survived. To be told that a culture's favorite sins like infanticide, sexual licentiousness,

---

20. Bizot, "My Savior, Their Killer"; cited in Strobel, *Case for Grace*, 100.
21. Strobel, *Case for Grace*, 102.

Part II: Bad Religion?

and gladiatorial bloodlust were evil made most people deeply opposed to the new religion. They saw the Christians' refusal to worship the emperor as just plain treason. Rome needed unity and the Christians were bringing division. The gods would bring disaster if they were not honored as they deserve. Larry Hurtado points out that devotion to the household deities was often integral to family life and worship of the pagan gods was so interwoven into society that their rejection was seen as a kind of atheism and crime against humanity. It was antisocial and subversive. Tacitus in the early second century called their crime "hatred of the human race."[22] So how did the church survive? Indeed, it not only survived but flourished.

There were several factors. For one thing, there was something of a turning away from popular mythology with its bickering, immoral, and puerile gods to the idea of a single good and noble God. This was especially true in some philosophical circles but the ideas also trickled down to the general population. The good and just Christian God, the God who sacrificed himself for us to bring us back to himself, not only fit this ideal but pushed it to an even higher level. There were also the *Pax Romana*, the era of peace in the Roman world, and the Roman roads, both of which facilitated transportation and communication and the spread of new ideas. But above all else, Christianity survived and grew because Christians valued and did good for all people and engendered the values of self-sacrifice.

Historian Tom Holland (who is not a Christian) says that his long time love of the noble Greeks and Romans ended as he came to understand their true ideals. "The longer I spent immersed in the study of classical antiquity, the more alien and unsettling I came to find it. The values of Leonidas, whose people had practiced a peculiarly murderous form of eugenics, and trained their young to kill uppity *Untermenschen* by night, were nothing that I recognized as my own; nor were those of Caesar, who was reported to have killed a million Gauls and enslaved a million more. It was not just the extremes of callousness that I came to find shocking, but the lack of a sense that the poor or the weak might have any intrinsic value." It is from Christianity, not the pagan world, that we "take for granted that it is nobler to suffer than to inflict suffering. It is why we generally assume that every human life is of equal value."[23]

Vincent Carroll and David Shiflett document much of the good that resulted from both the early and later spread of Christianity in their book

---

22 Tacitus *Annals* 15.44.5

23. Holland, "Why I Was Wrong About Christianity," *New Statesman*.

Christianity on Trial.[24] I will mention a few of their examples here and some more later. Dinesh D'Souza's book *What's So Great About Christianity* discusses similar historical examples but also looks more closely at some of the important philosophical implications of atheism and Christianity. I cannot recommend either book highly enough for anyone seeking to fully assess popular atheistic claims regarding the purported harm that results from religion.

Infanticide was widely accepted and practiced in the Greek and Roman world. Carroll and Shiflett tell how the church grew by rescuing abandoned children, often unwanted babies left to die of exposure. A couple of devastating plagues swept the Roman world. The first took a quarter to a third of the entire population in the second century of the Christian era. The second plague, a century later, may have taken two-thirds of the population of Alexandria alone. Pagans would often flee even their closest relatives and loved ones at the first sign of the disease, often leaving them to die in the streets. Christians would stay and nurse their own as well as complete strangers, greatly increasing their own risk of death. Non-Christians were astounded and impressed at this seemingly unnatural behavior.[25]

Carroll and Shiflett go on to mention the orphanages and hospitals Christians started, the thousands of widows and impoverished who were fed, and the thousands of homes for lepers throughout Europe and Asia that were built. Early Christians would fast and the money for the meals they had skipped would be set aside to feed the poor.

After Christianity was made the official religion, one Emperor, Julian, attempted to repress it. He tried to revive paganism and make it attractive again to the people. He ordered hospices be built to house strangers. He ordered that anyone be admitted and not merely other pagans, as was the normal practice. Otherwise they would be shamed, he said, by the "impious Galileans," the Christians, who "feed our people along with their own."[26] All of these charitable activities of the church flow from the high moral teachings of Jesus and the New Testament writers and from the strong motivation Christianity provides to follow these teachings. I will mention later some other beneficial social changes Christianity produced, particularly changes which benefited oppressed classes like women and slaves.

---

24. Much of Carroll and Shiflett's study follows the work of Rodney Stark, *The Rise of Christianity*.

25. Carroll and Shiflett, *Christianity on Trial*, 145.

26. Ibid., 146.

Part II: Bad Religion?

    I should mention one other reason the church flourished during the persecutions. Around the end of the second century, the church father, Tertullian, said the blood of the martyrs was the seed of the church. We have stories of Christian martyrs dying with such dedication to their Lord that sometimes once a person was killed another would step out of the crowd of observers, sometimes even a non-Christian, to confess Christ and to ask for the same privilege. In one account, after a number of executions, the crowd of pagan observers was deeply impressed at the fearlessness and steadfastness of the martyrs. One man, stunned at what he had seen could no longer hold in his admiration. "Great is the god of the Christians!" he cried out. The weary executioner turned, sword in hand, and quickly dispatched the speaker.

14

Biblical Discrimination and Oppression

BUT IF THIS MUCH good has come of Christianity, what about the evils many people think are intrinsic to the Christian teachings: anti-Semitism, oppression of women, homophobia; some will claim even slavery is advocated in Christian teaching. We will look at some of these claims next. We have already talked very generally about the Inquisition, pograms, and witch hunts. I think we should see by now that they cannot be blamed on Christianity but on the power of evil church leaders and followers. These were people who twisted the clear biblical teachings to fit their own desires. But our question now is, What of those whom Christianity specifically oppresses on the basis of teachings we find in the Bible? Or are there any people Christianity oppresses?

A Biblical View of Homosexuality

Practicing homosexuals are condemned in the Hebrew scripture which Christians accept (Lev 18:22; 20:13). And then the New Testament writer Paul also appears to have condemned homosexual practices (Rom 1:24–27; 1 Cor 6:9–10; 1 Tim 1:9–10). Should we see this as a kind of oppression of innocent people?

It is very questionable whether monogamous same-sex couples, if same-sex attraction is their most natural and irreversible disposition, are those Paul is condemning in Romans 1 (see especially 1:26–27). If Paul is rather criticizing opposite sex attracted people who seek same gender sexual relations simply because they are not content with normal monogamous heterosexual relations, this is also likely what he is describing and criticizing in the Corinthian and Timothy passages, if indeed he is there speaking of any kind of homosexual behavior at all. Thus it is difficult to see that any New Testament teaching condemns what might be called natural and monogamous same-sex intercourse. We will also see that the passages in the Hebrew scripture are even less helpful for determining the moral content of same gender sexual relations.

The first and most important passage we should look at which deals with this issue for a Christian understanding is Romans 1. Paul first says that God's wrath is revealed against people whom, despite their natural knowledge of God's existence and their moral obligations, God has finally given over to their evil desires (1:18–24). Since we are told that God patiently waits and draws us to God (Rom 2:4; 2 Pet 3:9), the passage indicates that these are people who have so strongly or constantly resisted this knowledge and sought to fulfill their sinful lusts that eventually God gives them up to their desires (see also 2 Thess 2:9–11). Notice that this passage also tells us that all people are aware of God's existence. This awareness may even be for only a very short period of time, at least long enough for the person to make some initial soul-deciding choices, and it may be in a form the individual may not even recognize as knowledge.

God gave them over to sexual impurity and to their desire to degrade their bodies with one another (1:24). Because they exchanged the truth for a lie (25), "God gave them up to degrading passions, for their women exchanged the natural function [or use] for that which is unnatural [or that which is in excess of the natural] (26), and in the same way also the men abandoned the natural function of the woman and burned in their desire toward one another" (27 NASB).

To say that they "exchanged" or "abandoned" the natural use of women for the unnatural means that they first must have been attracted to the natural use which they gave up. If not that, they at least were able to affirm or accept the "natural use" without any difficulty. Thus they sufficiently began with the opposite-sex attraction which they rejected. So to be given over to "degrading passions" means that they had normal opposite-sex passions or attractions which they then rejected and they knew that it was wrong for them to do so.

If we would try to imagine that Paul was allowing for the possibility that those who had only same-sex attraction to begin with be included among those who "gave themselves over to degrading passions," then the whole point of his argument fails. The point is that the wicked are guilty of willfully abandoning the natural knowledge and desires which should normally satisfy them. They are clearly guilty and deserving of judgment because they reject knowledge and attractions which they should have no trouble accepting. They know God exists and they know the moral law but resist this knowledge until God gives them over to their desires. They are without excuse (1:20, 32), something which cannot not be said about those who innately have only the same-sex attraction and have no access to normal heterosexual desires and are not in rebellion against God or their innate desires. So for the latter, whether given to them by heredity or environment, the same-sex attraction would be natural. The "shameful acts" men committed with other men (1:27), or women with other women, would not include monogamous same gender sex by those who are by nature same-sex attracted. It would not be for them shameful but natural.

John Boswell has most notably argued for this point though some, like Richard Hays, have attempted to refute him.[1] Interestingly, Hays points out that the notion of exchange is repeated within several verses. The rebellious *exchanged* the glory of God for idols of animals and humans (1:23). They *exchanged* the truth for a lie (1:25). Women *exchanged* the natural use for the unnatural (1:26). Men *abandoned* the natural use of women (1:27). He notes that "the deliberate repetition of the verb *metellaxan* ['exchange,' and similar verbs] forges a powerful rhetorical link between the rebellion against God and the 'shameless acts' (1:27, *RSV*)."[2] But it also shows that it is those who rebel against God and what God has given them who are the ones Paul is condemning. Paul is not condemning those who by nature are same-sex attracted and who are not in rebellion against God and what they are given.

It does not matter that Paul may have had no idea that, as Hays puts it, some people "have an inherent disposition toward same-sex erotic attraction." Hays comments that "the usual supposition of writers during the Hellenistic period was that homosexual behavior was the result of insatiable lust seeking novel and more challenging forms of self-gratification."[3] It seems clear that that this is what Paul is saying in verses 26–27 as well. It is only this kind of homosexual attraction and behavior that is being condemned in Romans 1. If Paul does not know of another kind of homosexual

---

1. Boswell, *Homosexuality*, 107–13; Hays, "Response to Boswell's," 184–215.
2. Hays, "Response to Boswell's," 192.
3. Ibid., 200.

Part II: Bad Religion?

orientation and behavior, or even if he does but just does not mention it, he *cannot* be taken to be condemning it.

Robert Gagnon argues that "the text . . . clearly implies that the 'degrading passions' to which God 'hands over' [1:26] are preexisting; and the 'leaving (behind)' [1:27] intimates awareness of some men who were (or had become) exclusively oriented to other males."[4] It clearly implies no such thing. Leaving behind or abandoning natural relations with women [1:27] more likely indicates that this, the desire for natural relations of men with women, was the original condition. Someone may have normal desires, leave those normal passions for degrading passions, and then God hands them over to those degrading passions, even passions which are exclusively same-sex.

Paul's reprimand of those who exchange the *natural* for the *unnatural* indicates that same-sex attraction should be avoided by those who have a choice in the matter as to their sexual orientation or attractions. His condemnation of those who are not satisfied with their natural opposite attracted orientation shows that they should and can be satisfied with it. He makes it clear that they are guilty and obviously deserve condemnation. This is not something that can be said of those who have no power to leave or suppress their same-sex attraction.

In the Corinthians and Timothy passages (1 Cor 6:9–10; 1 Tim 1:9–10) Paul uses one word which has been taken to indicate homosexual activity (*arsenakoitai*) which he condemns. It is very difficult to see that this word means anything other than sexually immoral men or possibly even male prostitutes (who cater to women as well as men).[5] Another term in the Corinthians passage, *malacoi*, though now commonly taken to speak of a passive homosexual partner, cannot be shown to more likely mean anything other than those who easily give in to temptation to sin.[6]

The writers after the time of Paul who used these terms or the passages containing these terms rarely indicated they meant anything close to normal homosexual behavior. Those who spoke of homosexual behavior did not use these terms or refer to these passages. As late as the twelfth century, Peter Cantor did not see these terms or passages as referring to general homosexuality.[7] Boswell claims that it was not until the ninth century, long

---

4. Gagnon, *Homosexual Practice*, 389.
5. Boswell, *Homosexuality*, 338–39, 341–53.
6. Ibid., 338–41.
7. Ibid., 349.

after these words had lost much of their original meaning, that we have a clear record of these terms referring to homosexual practices other than male prostitution. And even then, they carry some sense of prostitution as well.[8]

Robin Scroggs has argued that Paul used arsenakoitai as a composite word for the literal translation of the two Hebrew words in Leviticus 18:22 and 20:13 which mean *a man who has sex with a man*. These passages are the only ones which clearly condemn homosexual behavior in the Hebrew scripture. Scroggs argues that Paul or (more likely) some earlier Helenistic Jews made up the term to refer to any male/male sex and not necessarily a form of prostitution. If Paul did not coin the word, this would have been well understood in first-century Helenistic Jewish circles.[9]

Whether or not Paul did coin the word, it should have been understood by his Corinthian and Ephesian readers (Timothy was at Ephesus) as applying to general male/male sex. Whoever did coin the word, we need to ask why we have so few people for centuries after Paul thinking it meant this. If the churches at Ephesus and Corinth understood a general same-sex meaning for both terms, how could these meanings have been so quickly and so often confused with other meanings? (If someone other than Paul is the author of the book of Timothy, the same problem arises.) Paul would not have used terms he thought his readers probably did not know. If he was the author of both letters, he even used one of the terms in both. Wouldn't someone have passed on the same-sex meaning if that was the original readers' understanding? My argument here is not conclusive and it is not crucial to my overall argument but it seems to me that it is simply not at all likely that Paul was speaking of general homosexual activity in these passages.

I mentioned above that only two passages in the Hebrew scripture do clearly speak of and condemn male same gender sex. I will argue that there is nothing in these passages to indicate that it is morally harmful or, for any non-Jews, deserving of judgment. For such an argument one must look elsewhere.

It is often pointed out that morally neutral activity like working on the Sabbath or eating the meat of ceremonially unclean animals or wearing clothing made of mixed fabrics (say cotton and linen woven together) was

---

8. Ibid., 353.

9. Scroggs, *New Testament and Homosexuality*, 14, 83, 86, 107–9. Cf. Wright, "Homosexuals or Prostitutes?" 125–53.

condemned and violation of some of these laws even required the death penalty. Shouldn't same gender sex be seen as the same kind of morally neutral activity, activity condemned but not because it is morally harmful? But same gender sex is clearly a moral activity like theft or adultery which is also condemned whereas the previously mentioned activities are not moral activities. So if homosexual behavior is condemned in the Hebrew scripture because of its moral content, we should think that all people should see it as morally harmful. Does the Mosaic law condemn same gender sex because of its moral content?

The ceremonial and non-moral laws were not obligatory to anyone other than the Israelites. (Gentiles sojourning in Israel were obligated to keep some of these laws. But they were not obligated to keep them for moral reasons.) They were not obligatory to the Israelites because someone would be harmed if someone failed to keep them but because God commanded them and God should be obeyed. God gave these laws because they have symbolic meanings. Clothing made of mixed fabrics may symbolize mixing of righteous Israelites and the unrighteous pagans, for example. In the Mosaic covenant the people were to obey all of these laws, the symbolic as well as the moral, in exchange for God's promise of protection and prosperity. Gentile Christians are obligated to obey only the moral laws of the Hebrew scripture which prohibit harming others or which in some way usurp God's rightful place. These are laws we know are right because we see that disobeying them is clearly morally harmful. All people would be obligated to obey such laws, laws such as those condemning murder, adultery, or theft.

Now some Mosaic laws may prohibit certain behavior because they are morally harmful though only God is aware of the harm that results. It may not be obvious to us what harm they produce. So same gender sex might be morally harmful in this way. If we have good reason to think that God sees the harm that results though we do not, all Gentile Christians and other non-Jews should for this reason avoid it. But do we have reason to think this is true? We need to look closely at the two passages in the law of Moses which speak of homosexual behavior.

Leviticus 18:22 and 20:13 are the two passages which speak of male/male sex, each of which says this is detestable to God. The King James says this is an "abomination." The latter passage says the guilty couple must be killed. Chapter 18 says they are to be cut off, which usually means they are to be killed. In Leviticus 18, same gender sex is included in a list of a number of activities (vv. 6–23) all of which are said to be "detestable" to

Biblical Discrimination and Oppression

God (26–29). All of these condemned activities are sexual in nature except one. Most are incestuous relations.

A man having sex with his mother, step-mother, sister, half-sister, grand-daughter, father's sister, mother's sister, father's brother's wife, daughter-in-law, and brother's wife are the incestuous prohibitions. Other condemned and "abominable" sexual acts, some of which have incestuous features, include a man having sex with a menstruating woman, a woman and her daughter or granddaughter, a woman and her sister while both are alive, any other man's wife, a man, and an animal. The one condemned non-sexual activity is child sacrifice. Some of these are clearly morally wrong in almost any conceivable situation. The one most obviously and unquestionably *abominable* in our modern understanding of the word is child sacrifice.

However, looking at this list we may notice a problem. Abraham, the one man in the Bible who is said to be God's friend, certainly someone the Bible esteems as possibly the most righteous of all it describes, was married to his half-sister (Gen 20:12). Was he abominable or detestable in God's sight? Obviously not. The only reason we know of that this kind of marriage was made illegal by the time of Moses was because of the genetic harm it produces. Children of couples who are too closely related are more likely to have genetic handicaps or the couple will be sterile. If this is carried on for more than a few generations, the line will become extinct. Otherwise such marriages are not morally harmful.

Abraham's grandson, Jacob, was married to two sisters (Gen 29:16–28), another practice said to be detestable to God in Leviticus 18. Nothing in the scripture indicates that he was under God's curse for this. We might speculate that the hardship and internal family rivalry this brought to Jacob was one of the reasons marriage to two sisters was condemned in Leviticus 18. But there appears to be nothing otherwise intrinsically morally wrong with Jacob's marriage other than that it was polygamous. Polygamy was not condemned in the Hebrew scripture. Rather, it is an implication of Jesus' teachings that shows us it should be avoided.

Abraham's marriage was not intrinsically morally wrong. The law condemning such marriages would be little different from those prohibiting mixed fabrics in one's clothing. It is essentially an arbitrary law in God's sight. The law against marrying a half-sister at this stage in history was certainly necessary because of genetic reasons. Jacob's marriage was harmful and thus morally objectionable but only to a minor degree. It was likely important to eliminate the kind of rivalry which occurred in Jacob's family.

Part II: Bad Religion?

But someone who disobeyed either law, so long as no physical or social harm was done, was not an abomination in God's sight.

I could go on to talk about remarrying one's divorced wife who had remarried and then was divorced from her second husband (Deut 24:1–4) or a woman wearing men's clothing (22:5) or a man having sex with a menstruating woman (Lev 18:19), all of which were said to be abominations. But I think I can easily make my point without bringing up any of these other examples.

Now if disobeying some of the laws on the Leviticus 18 list is quite obviously detestable or abominable but others quite clearly are not, and yet if this chapter tells us that they *all* are, then the word used for "abominable" or "detestable" does not mean that at all. It means that God did not desire the Israelites to any longer participate in any such behavior, but they are not *all* truly detestable.

Some activities like child sacrifice are indeed abominations to God in the strongest sense we can imagine. It is for these that the writer says the earth vomited the people out (18:25, 27–28); they were sickening to God as they should be to anyone. But other than the ones we definitely know to be abominations and the ones we definitely know are not, how can we know in what category the others fit? We cannot. It follows that the Hebrew scripture cannot tell us anything about the moral content of same gender sexual relations. We cannot know it to be certain or even likely to be morally detestable to God. We only know that it is a proscribed activity, an activity the Israelites were to no longer practice. Possibly it was no different to God than Abraham's marriage to his half-sister. Since *we do not know* that disobeying the Mosaic law proscribing male/male sex is or is not morally harmful (given the Mosaic law alone), we cannot consider this a law a Gentile Christian or any other non-Jewish person is obligated to follow.

By claiming that the Bible does not condemn monogamous same gender sexual relations for constitutionally same-sex attracted individuals, there are certain things I am not saying. I am not saying that no same-sex attracted people should seek to become opposite sex attracted. Many have claimed to be able to change their same-sex attraction with proper counseling or therapy and no one should be denied the right to seek such therapy if they so choose.[10] Certainly there are some very bizarre and extreme therapies out there but that does not also mean that there are no very sane and, for many people, effective therapies.

10. Satinover, *Homosexuality and the Politics of Truth*, 168–209, chaps. 11–13.

BIBLICAL DISCRIMINATION AND OPPRESSION

And I am not saying that constitutionally same-sex attracted individuals who seek to be followers of Jesus should consider themselves free to pursue monogamous same gender sexual relations just because the scripture does not clearly condemn it. This is something each person should determine for him or herself as they search the scripture and call upon God to know what God would say to them. The gay person who comes to Christ should not fear God's anger or rejection. Jesus said that those who come to him he will by no means cast out (John 6:37). If we accept whatever we conclude he asks of us, he will give us the power to do it. It is so much better to find and know and love our God and creator than to hide from him because we are afraid of what he will ask of us.

Transgender Identity

A related issue, transgender identity, is not condemned or even discussed in scripture. The closest we get is a statement in the Deuteronomy 22:5 that men or women should not wear clothes of the opposite sex. This passage, like the ones condemning homosexual activity, cannot be shown to be in any way morally binding for anyone other than those under the Mosaic covenant. What we do know is that "[70% to] 98% of gender confused boys and [50% to] 88% of gender confused girls eventually accept their biological sex after naturally passing through puberty."[11] Opposite sex identified individuals should simply wait until puberty or possibly even longer before strongly affirming a gender identity other than their biological sex. They definitely should not seek or be offered cross-sex hormones or surgery for the purpose of sex reassignment until this time.

Even those who do finally strongly identify as transgender should be very cautious of such radical measures. As well as the health risk associated with cross-sex hormones (heart disease, stroke, diabetes, cancer, etc.), the suicide rate for adults who seek such treatment and surgery is twenty times higher than the general population. This suicide rate is not likely a result of transgender or homophobic oppression or discrimination since these numbers appear even in studies in Sweden, one of the most strongly LGBQT affirming countries. If at all available, transgender and gender identity confused children, teens, and young adults need compassionate counseling. What they do not need, especially from Christians, is condemnation.

---

11. A position statement from the American College of Pediatricians.

Part II: Bad Religion?

Christianity and Oppression

Christians who think all same gender sexual activity or transgender identity is morally wrong would not (or should not) seek anyone's harm. A little earlier I had argued that Christians, so far as they seek to follow the teachings of the Bible, cannot partake in social oppression, but perhaps a little more should be said. It is unimaginable that Jesus or Paul or any of Jesus' direct disciples could attempt to harm anyone. There are instances in the New Testament where Peter and Paul spoke a judgment which was determined by God (Acts 5:1–7; 13:8–11) but we have no evidence of Jesus' followers seeking on their own initiative to do anyone harm. Paul clearly warns against such actions (Rom 12:19). This is what it means to do to others as you would have done to yourself, to love your neighbor as yourself, and to do good to those who hate you (Matt 5:44–47; 7:12; 22:38–39; 25:40). Even when Jesus drove money-changers and those who sold sacrificial animals out of the temple and overturned their tables (Mark 11:15–17; John 2:13–17), it is unlikely that anyone was actually hurt. There was strong popular opposition to this kind of dishonest commerce since it was done in the temple area and many people, usually non-native Jews, had no choice but to pay unreasonable and exorbitant charges.

Jesus' refusal to condemn a woman caught in adultery teaches us that we must no longer seek to punish those who commit such sins.[12] If there is any punishment, it will have to come from God's hand in either this life or the next. In the Christian view, there should be no economic or significant social sanctions against gays just as there should be no such sanctions against those who commit unquestionable sexual sins—unless, of course, their actions do undeniably cause someone harm or usurp their rights.

Jesus said that anyone who relaxes or abolishes the least law of Moses will be called least in God's Kingdom and not the smallest stroke of a letter of the law will pass away (Matt 5:18–20). Wouldn't this mean that

---

12. This story in John 7:53—8:11 is not found in the earliest copies of the Gospels though there is good reason to believe the event or something very much like it did occur. It corresponds with Jesus' other teachings we have just mentioned. Moreover, since the postapostolic church so often required harsh punishment or penance for Christians involved in sexual sin, a story of Jesus forgiving someone without requiring any punishment would make this an account church leaders might hope had never been known. Leon Morris says "it scarcely could have been composed in the early church with its sternness about sexual sin" (*Gospel according to John*, 779). Augustine made the very reasonable suggestion that this story was kept out of the Gospels because some early leaders thought it would encourage sin.

his followers should strictly keep all the old laws, exposing and stoning adulterers, practicing homosexuals, and idolators even if they are our closest loved ones (see Deut 13:6, 8–15)? No, when we look at how Jesus dealt with such laws we discover that the way we are to keep them is by fulfilling their purpose, not by necessarily following them to the letter.[13] The scribes and Pharisees followed them to the letter and Jesus had just said that our righteousness must exceed theirs or we will not make it into God's kingdom (Matt 5:20).

Jesus, speaking specifically to his Jewish followers and opponents, said that the Sabbath law and similar laws need not be followed if greater harm would result from their observation (Mark 2:23–28). The purpose of the Sabbath law is to give us rest, it is not meant to simply be slavishly followed (see Deut 5:14–15). This is how his Jewish followers were to keep these laws. Likewise they need not strictly follow the dietary laws if circumstances hinder them since he said that no certain foods actually defile a person (Mark 7:5, 14–23). They are to be kept more by understanding their significance: they teach us the need to distinguish between the good and the evil and to avoid the evil.

Gentile followers of Jesus are not bound to keep anything of the Mosaic law other than the moral laws. They are not bound to keep any of the non-moral and symbolic laws like circumcision or the dietary laws so long as they understand their meaning and in that way fulfill their purpose. In this way one can say that even for Gentile Christians not one letter has passed from the law of Moses. Non-Jewish follower are obligated to keep moral laws like the law prohibiting adultery. We have seen that for both Gentile and Jewish followers of Jesus the death penalty for adultery is done away with. What remains of this law (that which will not pass away) is to recognize the gravity of the sin and to seek to avoid it.

Another possible understanding of Matthew 5 is that when Jesus says that some will be called least in the kingdom of heaven who relax any lesser law, it is only the scribes and Pharisees and their followers who call such people least, and those scribes and Pharisees are mistaken. Thus it may be that Jesus rightly relaxed or altered certain laws from the way they were originally understood. Still, not a letter of the law has passed away. The true meaning of each one remains and should be followed according to its meaning.

---

13. Bruce, *Hard Sayings of Jesus*, 42–48.

PART II: BAD RELIGION?

Jewish and non-Jewish Christians have no reason to follow laws requiring death or punishment for those who break the non-moral Mosaic law, laws which denigrate God (e.g, laws condemning idolatry and blaspheme), or even other moral laws—unless someone's actions do undeniably cause someone harm or usurp the rights of others.

Whether or not I am correct about the biblical understanding of homosexual behavior and sexual desire, it cannot be denied that certain behavior, like same-sex promiscuous sexual relations, is condemned. Christians would tell anyone who participates in such activity that they are doing wrong just as they must tell promiscuous heterosexuals that they are doing wrong. And they should also be excluded from Christian fellowship if they do not repent and this behavior continues. Of course this may make the reprimanded person feel badly, but if they are truly harming someone, possibly including themselves, such a rebuke would be needed. On the possibility that someone is unknowingly harming someone, they should certainly be confronted with evidence that they are. This should not be seen as oppression or wanton discrimination.

All religions and world views hold some behavior to be harmful and often there is great disagreement as to which is or is not injurious. Surely our greatest human right is the right to search out and determine truth for ourselves. For any two people to disagree as to whether a particular thinking or behavior is harmful is an inevitable outcome of our exercising this right. Disagreement is such an important good for human societies that this good far outweighs any harm which may also result. Without free speech and free access to information (we cannot have the latter without free speech), we cannot determine truth for ourselves. Without these freedoms a select few determine what all must believe. Free speech should not be constrained unless it is libelous or results in undeserved physical, economic, or other clear and overriding harm to another person. But so-called *hate speech* laws should not be allowed to censor anyone who merely tells someone that they are acting wrongly or are harming themselves or someone else. Since all people should be allowed the right to determine if such claims are true, they should never be silenced or censored.

Is Christianity Inherently Intolerant?

A major reason Friedrich Nietzsche rejected his Christian background was his perception of Christianity's resentment or hatred of the world. With its

Biblical Discrimination and Oppression

exclusivism Christians are to shake the dust off of their feet of the towns which reject their message (Mark 6:11). All who reject Christianity are rejected. The towns which did not repent at Jesus' teaching he consigned to hell (Matt 11:20–24).

By maligning Christianity for teachings like these, Nietzsche missed the context and thus an accurate understanding of these passages. Jesus' teachings in these towns were, according to the passages, accompanied by undeniable miracles. The point was that this was a willful disregard for sure and overpowering evidence. This is the height of arrogance. It is a willful indulgence in irrationality which allows one to disbelieve exactly what one wants to disbelieve.

Today, should someone bring the Christian message to those who have not yet heard, the people may not confront the same miraculous evidence Jesus or his disciples demonstrated but they certainly should hear the message on just the chance that these claims are true. If we know ourselves to be people who willfully bring harm to others, then we know that if there is a holy God, we are alienated from him. Yet the Christian message tells us that Jesus can provide for us the reconciliation we need. If the only way we can find fulfillment and completion is by finding this relationship with God and having these sins removed (as their message claims), it would be reprehensible for anyone to not even consider this message. This does indeed result in a kind of Christian animosity toward the world (those who unreasonably reject the Christian message), but an animosity they clearly deserve. Christian animosity toward the world in this sense has nothing to do with oppression or causing harm to others or even hating the world. One can still love people while pitying and even being angry with them. In turn, Nietzsche's animosity toward Christianity appears to be completely undeserved.

Christians do not reject all who reject Christianity. All who reject it who know it is true certainly should be reprimanded. Christians would say that generally all who will not even consider it will likewise face God's judgment. But all who reject it after honestly evaluating it are not rejected by God. Of course, honest evaluation must also include seeking God, calling upon God for the truth. Jesus taught that any who seek God in this way and continue to do so will eventually find that Christianity is true (John 7:17; Acts 10:34–35; 17:27). The point is that those who honestly evaluate and reject Christianity will not reject it forever.

15

Does Religion Promote Superstition?

CONTINUING OUR DISCUSSION OF whether biblical teachings promote the oppression of innocent people, we should now look at the claim that Christianity promotes superstition while a secular world view does not. An old story, likely from after the Middle Ages, may provide us a good starting point to look at this claim. A certain elderly lady was not invited to a local village festival. Perhaps she was simply not told of the event. She happened to come into town when the festival was in progress and became visibly angry when she saw she had been slighted. As soon as she left, an immense storm arose and the people concluded the woman must have been a witch and caused the storm. Authorities were notified who then tortured her to confess and later she was executed as a witch.

Now this supposedly took place in the context of a claimed Christian culture. But if these people were Christians, they could not be persecuting witches in the first place. Jesus taught that we cannot do that. So they were not really Christians at all, or possibly they were Christians in some vague or nominal sense of the word but they were very distant from the teachings of Jesus and his direct followers. For example, we have just looked at Jesus' teaching that adultery should not be a capital offense as the law of Moses commands (John 7:53–8:11). This and similar teachings indicate that not all capital crimes in the Hebrew scripture should continue to be held as such. Only those laws should continue which our natural moral awareness tells us should continue, e.g., punishment for murder. Also the use of torture to obtain confessions for crimes or heresy certainly does not follow from any biblical teachings. Such practices certainly oppose all that

Jesus and his first followers taught. Nevertheless, even if it was believed that witches were harmful to society and deserving of death, some kind of religious belief, however opposed to New Testament teachings, was at core responsible for this belief.

But notice that secularism has the same problem. Hitler searched for Jews to kill them; Pol Pot searched out intellectuals and murdered them. Both were secular witch hunts. Both offered nonreligious reasons for thinking these people were destroying their societies and they both tried to indoctrinate their people to believe it. (Hitler and his propagandists did also offer religious reasons though it is more likely that both he and they did not accept these reasons but gave them only to appeal to popular prejudice.) One cannot point to witch hunters who claimed to be Christians as an example of a religion which produces superstition without admitting that secularism produces its own superstitions. The answer to both kinds of witch hunts is to rationally assess the various claims that are made. Are the witches or Jews or intellectuals truly causing harm to anyone and deserving of this treatment?

Secondly, whether or not the people in the first example could call themselves Christians, if they were reasonable they should have accepted that it was more likely a coincidence that the storm arose as quickly as it did than that the old woman was a witch and she caused it. So here, even assuming that witches exist who can cause storms, we can make rational judgments that would end much unnecessary harm. If the old woman had raised her hands and cried out to the sky and suddenly a storm of hurricane force arose, then we would have better reason to think she actually was someone with supernatural powers. But even then, we would not have reason to do her harm.

Some may have the irrational belief that a particular person is a witch who should be killed and others could likewise have irrational secular beliefs like the belief that blood-letting can heal. Unless both beliefs are based on a rational assessment of evidence, they are both superstitions.

Or consider the ancient myths that are held up as examples of religious superstition, foolish beliefs about the world that purely secular and rational science has supposedly destroyed. Are these not clear examples of how we advance as we leave religion behind? No, because many of these myths are actually secular myths. Consider the stories of how giant, invisible wolves or dragons devour the sun during an eclipse. These are natural beings who inhabit the physical world like wolves in the wild, not an eternal

God or even gods. Certainly just because they are invisible does not make them religious beings. Scientists admit that everything from electrons to dark matter to black holes cannot be seen. Even the air that surrounds us is invisible to us.

In one Norse creation myth the first life, a mortal giant from whom came other giants, mortal gods, humans, and the world itself, was created as ice and cold met and mixed with volcanic fires. In a Chinese creation myth chaos gave birth to an egg in which a giant, mortal humanoid formed whose body eventually gave substance to some of the features of the earth. These are purely secular myths of the same kind as we hear discussed today when biologists talk about life emerging from a prebiotic soup or when cosmologists talk about the Big Bang evolving from a chaotic sea of vacuum energy. They are all the same *kind* of creation story. Some may just happen to have a degree of plausibility given our present scientific knowledge while others have none.

Some ancient secular beliefs have been confirmed and are still with us (though usually they are now quite a bit different from their original form, e.g., the atomic theory of matter) but likewise some ancient religious beliefs have been substantiated by scientific advances (e.g., belief that the earth is suspended in space, Job 26:7). Religious beliefs do not foster superstition or suffering any more than secular belief. The problems arise when those religious and secular beliefs are not rationally justified. We have no good evidence that religious people tend to produce more superstitions and false beliefs than nonreligious people, and it certainly cannot be shown that they produce such beliefs because they are less intelligent.[1]

---

1. An important long term demographic study in America (Murray, *Coming Apart*) indicates that religious people generally tend to be more intelligent than the nonreligious. See Jensen, "Einstein's Religion," for discussion of this and other studies.

16

Hard Hearts and Bad Laws

THE HEBREW SCRIPTURE HAS some laws which seem almost trite and meaningless, yet if they were violated one could have expected the harshest punishments. They seem unworthy of a good God. For example, people could be executed for merely picking up fire wood on the Sabbath (Num 15:32–36). How can such laws be justified? And if they cannot be justified, do Christians who accept the Bible tacitly approve such oppressive laws?

Sabbath Laws

In the case of the Sabbath law we need to first remember that the Hebrew scripture tells us that the Israelites had made a covenant, a mutual agreement with God. They believed that they had accepted God's offer that if they would keep his laws and worship and serve him only, he would protect and prosper them and they would be his specially chosen people. They were told that God had commanded them to keep the seventh day of the week by not working on that day (Exod 31:12–17). This was one of the special signs of obedience to God's covenant so to break this law was hardly a trivial action. For most of Israel's history those who wished to be free of the covenant had opportunity to leave this country but they knew the consequences of disobeying these laws if they were to stay. If they were to work on the seventh day in flagrant disobedience, they would have only themselves to blame for their deaths. And again, with the coming of Jesus' teachings the idea of strict adherence to the letter of the law was also superseded.

PART II: BAD RELIGION?

There are other laws and apparent commands from God which at first appearance seem to be morally harmful. Could a good God have commanded evil laws? Many of the problems some of these laws raise can be resolved by recalling Jesus' statement that some laws were allowed because of the hardness of the people's hearts. The example Jesus dealt with involved divorce. He said that in the Mosaic law God allowed divorce for other than sexual sin because of the hardness of the people's hearts (Matt 19:8). They were unwilling to control their lust or to love and stay with just one person for their entire lives.

The Law of Warfare

One example to which we might apply Jesus' statement was the law of warfare. God told the Israelites that when attacking a city, first ask them to surrender. If they do, the captives should all be consigned to forced labor. Presumably this only involved the men, and families would not be disrupted. If they do not surrender and are then captured, they are to kill all the adult men and enslave all the women and children (Deut 20:10–17). How, we might ask, can such a law come from a good God who loves all people?

We first need to understand that these enemies were not the Canaanites whose land the Israelites were invading. God had said the Canaanites should be completely destroyed. This is a distinct problem we will deal with later. These were other surrounding nations with whom the Israelites were to seek to live in peace. Israel would thus be fighting in self-defense any other nation or city attacking them. The threat of killing all the men from a city which would not surrender and enslaving the rest would strongly motivate the city to surrender. But more importantly, it may be that the only way they could deal with such aggressors was to make and carry out this kind of threat. If a conquered city did not have its population of fighting men removed, it would rise up at a later time to attack Israel again. So something like this procedure may have been necessary to prevent greater bloodshed. We do not know that modern laws of warfare could have been adapted at this time in history. We may have good reason to doubt that they would have worked.

But let's suppose that modern and more ethical laws of war could have worked. Perhaps the men could have been imprisoned and eventually released rather than enslaved or killed. Suppose the women and children need not have been enslaved. If that were true, then this Israelite law of war may have been allowed by God because of "the hardness of [the people's] hearts." It was a lesser-of-two-evils law. God allowed it because the people were not willing to be even this humane to a people who wanted to destroy them. The Mosaic law of war was more humane than what the Israelites would have done without this law, yet they would not have accepted any law more humane than the Mosaic law.

17

Women and the Bible

CONTINUING OUR LOOK AT biblical teachings which have been accused of promoting the oppression of innocent people, we should look at some which are claimed to advocate harming or denigrating women. After looking at some of these passages and claims we should also look at some of the ways women's conditions changed under Christianity.

Rape and Forced Marriage

One of the Mosaic laws says that if a man rapes an unbetrothed virgin he must marry her (Deut 22:28–29). This sounds like an unjust law forcing marriage upon the victim. In the case of a seduction, the man must also marry the woman unless her father refuses (Exod 22:16–17). Whether they marry or not he must pay the father a brideprice. For rape, he must also pay the father a brideprice, in this case an enormous amount equal to five times the standard annual wage, and he can never divorce the woman.[1] A marriage like this would provide the woman financial security for life. (If the man cannot pay the brideprice, he must sell himself as a slave, likely directly to the father; not an enviable condition for someone who has seduced, or worse, raped, his master's daughter.)

These were casuistic laws, laws given as examples for other cases. Therefore, because the father can refuse the marriage in the case of a seduction, likely he can do so in the case of a rape as well. And if the father

---

1. Walton, *Bible Background Commentary: Old Testament*, 196.

can do so, very possibly the woman can also refuse the marriage in the case of a rape or seduction. Also, because the rape of a virgin was seen as an enormous evil in this culture (Gen 34:7, 13, 25–27, 31), it is likely that other punishment was involved—perhaps something like the common forty lashes. (Even two or three lashes would likely be a good deterrent for rape.) Much was left to the discretion of the judges given the circumstances at the time.

Now I have just given the best possible reading of these texts and, I think, the most likely understanding. If I am completely wrong and this is in fact a law allowing mistreatment of women in a patriarchal and sometimes misogynous culture, then this would be another example of a law which was given because of the hardness of the people's hearts. It was not the best possible law but it was allowed because the more powerful male population would not allow a more humane or just law. Nevertheless, it was still better than if there were no such law. Without such laws clan wars or similar conflicts could easily result.

The key I want to emphasize is that if we do determine that a given law in the Hebrew scripture is harmful or unjust, very often this can be adequately explained as being allowed because of the hardness of the people's hearts.

Jesus' Opposition to Divorce

Some have pointed to Jesus' teaching against divorce as fostering harmful relationships. A woman cannot leave an abusive husband, they may say, because she can only divorce him on the grounds of adultery or similar sexual sin (Matt 5:31–32) and she should always forgive him (Matt 18:21–22). If he is physically abusive however, might this not put her life in danger?

David Instone-Brewer recounts an incident in which a woman was killed by a violently abusive husband. She would not have died had her church leaders not told her to return to her husband and trust God to make the marriage work. Instone-Brewer argues that such abuse *is* grounds for divorce under a fully biblical teachings even if adultery is not involved.[2] He

---

2. Instone-Brewer, *Jesus Scandals*, 132–46. The incident is recounted on page 140. If Instone-Brewer is correct, my statement in the following discussion would not be accurate. The Bible would allow for divorce in cases of abuse and certain other forms of marital neglect but not for virtually any reason whatsoever. Paul also takes it for granted that adultery is grounds for divorce.

presents a very strong biblical argument but whether he is correct or not, it should be very clear to anyone reading Jesus' teachings that Jesus never said one should not leave an abusive relationship. This should be obvious. The church leaders who were responsible for this woman's death went far beyond Jesus' teachings in their own excessive opposition to divorce.

Divorce is not the same as separation. Separation without the intent to remarry is not precluded in the New Testament when adultery is not involved. There is nothing in the New Testament that says a wife must physically remain with her husband. And there is no contradiction in the actions of forgiving someone while at the same time keeping away from them. Paul does say that one must not separate from one's spouse, but in this case he clearly means divorce (1 Cor 7:10) since in Roman law separation was equivalent to divorce. So Paul was saying that if one does separate (such as for abuse), one must not consider it a divorce and may not marry another. And the separated couple should seek reconciliation (7:11) but only so long as it is certain that no possible danger is involved.

Women in Paul's Teaching

There are several New Testament statements which are often taken as indicating a subservience of women to men. Before concluding that the New Testament teaches a low view of women, we should look at these passages carefully.

In 1 Corinthians 11:3 Paul says that man is the head of woman as God is the head of Christ and Christ the head of man. Manfred Brauch points out that the Greek term for head *never* means an authority over another person. It can mean "origin," "source," "starting point," "crown," "completion," or "consummation." He shows that the more likely meaning of Paul's statement is that man is the source and origin of woman.[3] Paul's statement likely reflects the creation story in Genesis 2 which indicates that the first woman came from the first man.

Again Paul says that women should be silent in the church (1 Cor 14:34) and that this command is from God (14:37). Does this indicate a prejudice against women or special privileges for men over women among Christians?

In the early church, after someone lectured or perhaps even during the time of instruction there may have been some time for questions and

3. Brauch, *Hard Sayings of Paul*, 134–40, chap. 22.

discussion. Craig Keener points out that because women were generally less educated than men at this time, they were more apt to ask simplistic or even ignorant questions than the more informed men, and asking such questions was perceived as rude and thus shameful (14:35b). Lecturers at this time willingly accepted intelligent questions. So Paul says women should ask their husbands their questions when they are home (14:35a) rather than raise them after or during the time of instruction.[4]

Paul clearly recognized that women do worship aloud, prophesy aloud, and pray aloud in the worship services (see Acts 2:4, 17–18; 21:8–9; 1 Cor 11:5). So it is very difficult to deny that men and women alike participated not only in these verbal activities but also in the full list of vocal gifts he describes which he says should all be present in the church. These include giving a prophetic word from God, a tongue, an interpretation of a tongue, a teaching, and a song (1 Cor 14:26). (A tongue was a message in an unknown or a spiritual language given by God to a person to be interpreted by the speaker or someone else.) Notice that he says that "each" person has one of these spoken words or gifts to share. He addresses his readers as "brothers" yet it is understood that he is speaking to both men and women.

It seems likely then that when Paul says that women should be silent in the church meeting, that they must be in submission, and that it is disgraceful for a woman to speak in church, he is likely referring to this discussion or question and answer period. They are in submission only in the sense that they should not speak at this time.

Paul says this submission is commanded in the law (1 Cor 14:34) and also that this is the Lord's command (14:37). We do not know of any statement from Jesus to this effect and we do not know what law Paul may be referring to. Possibly this information was given to Paul by direct revelation as he says his basic knowledge of Christianity was given to him (Gal 1:11–12). So he is likely referring simply to the need for order which would not be possible if the discussion time is filled with naive or foolish questions. The Mosaic law obviously assumes an orderly time of ritual and worship. This may be what Paul means when he says the law requires women to be in submission. They should be quiet at this time whether or not they have been causing disorder.

Notice also that women may at some times be the ones giving the lecture or instruction (1 Cor 14:26). At least we should think this, were it not for another statement Paul made at a later time. Assuming that Timothy

---

4. Keener, *Bible Background Commentary, New Testament*, 483.

was written by Paul, he said he does not permit a woman to teach or have authority over a man (1 Tim 2:12). So Paul may not have allowed women to teach at Corinth either. However, another possibility is that since the letter to Timothy was written about eight to ten years latter than the one written to the Corinthians, this may instead indicate a change in Paul's view. With increased social pressure, he may have eventually decided that women should not publicly teach in the church. This would not have limited the other channels women had for benefiting or edifying the church: namely their exercise of prophecy, singing, spoken prayer, spoken worship, a tongue, or an interpretation.

We should look a little more closely at Paul's statement that he does not permit a woman to teach or have authority over a man (1 Tim 2:12). It is interesting that he says, "I do not permit . . ." making it clear that this is not necessarily a command for everyone in all possible situations and cultures. The Greek, Roman, and Jewish cultures at this time often simply did not allow women to speak in public. They particularly rejected women teachers and leaders. Paul may have thus been accommodating the cultural mores and laws so as not to excessively offend. He said he himself would even avoid ever eating meat if it would keep a Christian from being offended or a non-Christian from being closed to the gospel (1 Cor 8:13; 9:10–23). Flaunting disdain for accepted customs would only hinder the Christian message. Observers would only see what they take to be scandalous behavior and would miss the Christian message entirely. As Paul was willing to give up any right or privilege in order to honor Christ and avoid hindering Christianity's advancement, so he asked this of all believers. With this understanding, Christian women were more than willing to follow Paul's example.

Paul's very limited constraint on women speaking in church (during discussion during or following teaching) thus cannot be shown to be intended for all churches. It is indeed God's command, but it is God's command only for certain churches at this time because of their special cultural conditions. It is certainly not for all churches in all possible cultures and settings. And Paul's teaching that women should not teach or have authority over men is not presented as even a command from God, it was enjoined only to accommodate the norms and ethos of the time.

Brauch sees some other special conditions which may have been present in the Corinthian church and the church at Ephesus (the church with which Timothy was associated) which may have provided special reasons for commanding women to be silent during given portions of the church meeting.[5] Whether he is correct or not, we see that Paul's statements do not apply to all churches at all times. And some of his statements did not even apply to all of the churches of his time.

In another letter written about five years earlier than his letter to Timothy, Paul does say that women should submit to their husbands (Eph 5:22). But notice his actual wording. He says, "Be subject one to another out of reverence for Christ; [first,] wives to your husbands as to the Lord." He then goes on to show some of the ways husbands should be subject to their wives. He says husbands should love their wives as Christ loved the church enough to die for her. I added the bracketed word "first" to the above quotation because the structure of his statement suggests it. It appears as though he is saying, "Submit to one another. In marital relations let it be done under this pattern: first wives submit to your husbands, then husbands submit to your wives in the following manner." Paul is saying that husbands should so protect, esteem, cover, value, defend, shelter, and love their wives as to be willing to give up their lives for them (5:25).[6] As Christ became a servant to his followers, so the husband is to make himself a servant to his wife (John 13:14; Luke 22:25-27). As Jesus is not a domineering tyrant who lords over his church, so a husband is not to be domineering over his wife. He is to hear and compassionately consider all that his wife has to say. His deep love and care and deference for his wife makes her opinions and desires his deepest concern. He is to so honor and esteem his wife that he would give up anything in order to nurture and provide for her. Decisions are made mutually. The husband does not disregard the wife's opinion. This is mutual submission.

In Genesis 3:16 women were cursed to have husbands who would "rule over" them. But this cursed existence is a result of a broken relationship with God. In Christ the curse is broken as couples begin to live in biblical mutual submission.

Paul's message was that there is neither Greek nor Jew, male nor female, slave nor free, that we are all one is Christ, that class and social distinctions are erased for Christians (Gal 3:28; Col 3.11). This allowed for equal and complete participation by women and slaves and others in the church except for the special cases we have discussed. Christians understood that there was a complete equality of believers in God's sight and in

---

5. Brauch, *Hard Sayings of Paul*, 166–72, 252–57, chaps. 27, 44.
6. Ibid., 212–17, chap. 36.

principle in the function, offices, and ministries of the church. There was equality in principle as to who could fill those functions and offices.

Women clearly had the office of teacher in the early church, though it was often discretely relegated to private conversations. Aquila and his wife Priscilla both taught Apollos to bring him to a better understanding of Christianity (Acts 18:24–26). When they are mentioned in the New Testament, Priscilla's name is sometimes placed ahead of her husband's name suggesting that she may have been the more prominent teacher and evangelist of the two.

Some women had prominent leadership positions as leading officers (*prostatis*) and deacons (Rom 16:1–2), fellow workers with Paul (Rom 16:3; Phil 4:2–9), and even apostles (Rom 16:7, the most natural reading of this passage). This shows that early on women likely did have authority over men in some churches. In all churches some women were considered to equal or excel many of the men in their labors. From Paul's statement it appears that female leadership, other than merely over other women, was not practiced in the churches Paul founded though it may have been practiced in some others. Such leadership positions were lost to women in the coming centuries as the church lost sight of its original practices, became excessively influenced by Greek and Roman culture, and more universally accepted the Pauline pattern. Max Weber pointed out that stronger female participation generally diminishes after the earliest stages of a religion[7]

Lacking any cultural hindrances today in most of the Western world, nothing in the Bible indicates that women should not be allowed the full right to lead, preach, and teach in the church. Unconditional submission of women to men in the family, church, or society is done away with by the work of Christ; only mutual submission remains in the family, and leadership in church and society should be open to men and women alike.

Women's Conditions under Christianity

Alvin Schmidt argues that women's rights have advanced enormously under Christian influence.[8] Women in ancient Athens typically could not interact or eat with male guests, could not divorce their husbands, had virtually no freedom, and had the social status of slaves. Rarely were they educated and they were not allowed to speak in public. A son gave prestige to his parents

---

7. Weber, *Sociology of Religion*, 104.
8. Schmidt, *How Christianity Changed the World*, 97–124, chap. 4.

but a daughter was an economic and social burden. Unwanted children were commonly abandoned—females much more so than males. Abortion and infanticide were widely accepted and practiced.

Often Roman women in the first century could not divorce their husbands, they were restricted in their ability to inherit property, and usually only upper-class girls received a limited education. Men could execute their wives for adultery or, with approval from a tribunal, even lesser offenses. Men could legally kill adult children and grandchildren. Women could not speak in public and were restricted in what they could wear or how they could appear in public. A woman could be divorced for merely being in public without a veil. How strongly such laws and customs were enforced or exactly to whom they applied varied with the time and location.

Jewish women at this time could not speak in public or testify in court. Some rabbis taught that it was shameful to teach them the Law or to even greet a woman. A common prayer expressed gratitude one was not born a woman.

Besides evangelism, one reason the early church grew was because it did not practice abortion or infanticide and it did much to rescue abandoned babies. Not long after Christianity was officially tolerated in Rome, the thousand year old law giving a husband life and death power over his wife and children was repealed. Similar laws and customs also soon ended. Roman fathers often sold their daughters in marriage, sometimes at age twelve or younger. This changed as Christians normally married according to their own choice. The New Testament teachings of mutual submission and the special value husbands were to have for their wives allowed women in Christian families to benefit long before laws changed under the repressive Greek, Roman, and Jewish cultures.

The Qu'ran allows wives to be beaten and this is routinely accepted and practiced in many Muslim countries. In some Islamic countries women today may even be mutilated or killed by offended husbands.

So called female circumcision (clitoridectomy) is an unimaginably painful cutting away of genitalia in young girls still practiced in some Muslim countries in Africa and the Middle East. Western nations have outlawed such practices out of a moral revulsion ingrained from centuries of Christian influence.

India has long had the custom of *suttee*, burning a widow alive on her deceased husband's funeral pyre, sometimes with child-bride widows between five and fifteen. This officially ended with the British occupation.

The custom was present in other countries as well and has still continued illegally.

The thousand year old Chinese custom of foot binding ended early in the twentieth century largely through Christian influence. Chronically painful, it sometimes led to infection and death.

Had there been no Christianity, we would have inherited a very different moral sensitivity. Probably it would include something of the compassionless and pitiless ideals of the Greek, Roman, Celtic, or Nordic cultures. One has to wonder if any of these customs, so harmful to women, would have ended had Christianity never existed.

19

Slavery

CHRISTIANITY IS OFTEN ACCUSED of encouraging or at least passively accepting slavery. To assess such claims we should look at the biblical teachings. First we should consider slavery in ancient Israel.

To enslave an innocent person was made as a capital offense in Israel (e.g., Deut 24:7; cf. Gen 15:13–14) and it was recognized as a grave evil as well in the New Testament (1 Tim 1:9–10). Slaves in Israel were usually war captives or the poor who could not pay their debts. Israelite slaves were actually indentured servants who served only six years or until the year of Jubilee (every fifticth year), whichever came first. A foreign slave could be kept for their entire lifetime. If a poor man sold his daughter into slavery it was normally to be a wife, in which case she would not be freed after the usual six years. But then, except for the manner in which she became the man's wife, she would have essentially all the rights of a free woman (Exod 21:7–11).

Israelites were constantly reminded to be fair and compassionate to their slaves, the poor, and the aliens among them because, they must always remember, they too were once slaves in Egypt. Wealthy and poor, children and slaves, aliens and widows and orphans—all were to partake and rejoice as one in the festivals because, again, they were reminded that they were once slaves in Egypt. In this manner they were to recognize that no one person is ultimately higher than another (Deut 16:10–12; 24:17–22). Job said he dare not ignore his slave's grievance since it is God who formed both the slave and himself in the womb (Job 31:13–15). God saw them as equals, God saw them as being the same. How could he face his God with such a sin on his hands? he asked. The slave was thus to be seen and treated as essentially a hired worker and as one's equal.

For an Israelite to buy a foreign slave from passing traders was then to be seen as more of an act of kindness, saving the person from the mistreatment of a foreign master and oppressive foreign laws. Runaway Israelite and foreign slaves were not to be returned to their masters (Deut 23:15) probably since this would indicate mistreatment if the master was an Israelite. One had no obligation to return foreign slaves of foreign masters whether mistreatment was an issue or not. When Israelite slaves were freed, the master was to provide for them generously so they would have enough until they could make a living on their own (Deut 15:13–15). Foreign slaves were to be allowed a day of rest on the Sabbath and generally to be given the right to share in the festivals (Exod 20:10; 12:43–44).

One could punish a slave but not so much as to cause their immediate death. That would require the master's death (Exod 21:12; Gen 9:5–6).[1] If the slave did die but not immediately, this would indicate the killing was not intentional, in which case the master would not be punished (Exod 21:20–21). (There is some ambiguity in this passage since it may instead be saying that if the slave recovers completely, the master will not be punished.) A slave was not considered one's property. The above verse likely means merely that the slave represents the master's money or source of income. Otherwise, if the slave were literally considered one's property, there would have been no punishment at all for killing a slave. A punishment resulting in the loss of an eye, even the loss of a tooth, would require immediate freedom for the slave (21:26–27). Since these were casuistic laws, laws given for judges merely as examples, almost any other permanent injury to the slave, and likely some non-permanent injuries, would have required manumission as well.

I cannot touch on all of the special laws that apply to slaves but I would refer to Paul Copan's discussion for those wishing to pursue the topic in more detail.[2] For our purposes, we should understand that the slave in Israel was seen as essentially a hired worker, or at least that was God's command and intention. Of course what God commanded and what the people did were often two different things. Some Israelites and Jews mistreated

---

1. Tyler Vela does a more detailed study arguing this in " 'Slavery' In the Bible." He also argues that the slaves in Israel were not to be physically punished at all. Though he does offer a very strong argument, in the above I will assume that slaves could be physically punished though within very strict limits.

2. Copan, *Is God a Moral Monster?* 124–57, chaps. 12–14.

Slavery

or unlawfully took slaves or refused to release them when their time of service was over. The Bible says that these are some of the reasons their two kingdoms were eventually destroyed (Amos 2:6; 8:4, 6; Jer 34:12–21).

Laws such as these which were more beneficial to slaves would certainly mitigate the evil of slavery in Israel. Since this does not likely justify the practice in all of its aspects, we should recognize that some portions of the laws concerning slavery were, as Jesus said, allowed because of the hardness of the people's hearts. They could have had better laws but the people would not accept them.

During Jesus' time and following, slavery was deeply established and institutionalized in the Gentile world. New Testament writers like Paul could only encourage and help slaves to endure their lot unless or until they had opportunity to receive their freedom (1 Cor 7:21–23). Slaves in the Roman world could generally count on receiving their freedom by age thirty. Many sold themselves into slavery for economic, social, and educational advancement.[3] It was often a kind of apprenticeship in which they received specialized training and would eventually buy back their freedom. Of course not all Roman slavery was this good. There were also some who were slaves for life and many who lived and worked under very oppressive conditions. Slavery in the salt mines and the galleys was often the cruelest punishment short of execution the state could impose on perceived criminals and enemies.

Paul and the other early church leaders did not seek to overthrow the institution of slavery. That would have brought very strong and unnecessary social and political opposition to the early church and it would have diverted attention from the message Christians wanted to make. Because slavery was often merely a form of punishment for criminals, sometimes taking the place of our prison system today, and because so many sold themselves into slavery for economic and social advancement, these writers likely did not see it overall as the unspeakable evil it would become in other cultures, cultures like our own.

Paul encouraged slaves to obey their masters and to work honestly for them. They should take their freedom if they could get it and people should not seek to become slaves, which in some cases was a strong temptation for many people. He told masters to treat their slave with justice and fairness and emphasized their equality in God's sight (Eph 6:5–9; Col 3:22–25; Tit 2:9–10). Peter told slaves to obey and respect even unjust masters because

---

3. Bartchy, "Slavery," 545.

God honors those who endure unjust treatment (1 Pet 2:18–20). This could also be a witness to their masters of the power of God in their lives.

Slaves could became leaders in the church; many were highly esteemed as possessing special gifts which benefited God's kingdom (teachers, evangelists, pastors, prophets). Christian slaves and masters were seen as equals and would relate to each other in the church as equals.

Except for special conditions such as when someone may want to become a slave for economic and social advancement, Jesus' teachings that one should love one's neighbor as oneself and do to others as one would have done to oneself are incompatible with having another person as a slave. If I do to a slave as I would have done to myself, I must let them go free. So Peter and Paul's teachings were temporary measures for Christians to follow when the institution of slavery was unassailable. When Christians looked at the full implications of Jesus' teachings, they could not own slaves and eventually they would be able to seek political action to abolish slavery. In the Greco-Roman world Paul could not advocate the abolition of slavery. The time would come when Christians could do so without repercussions to the Christian outreach from the non-Christian world. It is noteworthy that the early modern abolitionist movements were primarily movements based on Christian principles and teachings. Often they were purely and ostensively Christian movements. It was because of what Christians read in the Bible that they saw that slavery is wrong.

19

Is the New Testament Anti-Semitic?

WE HAVE EARLIER LOOKED at the lives of Casper ten Boom and his family. By consistently seeking to follow the teachings of the New Testament, they endured enormous suffering in German concentration camps, some even endured death, to protect persecuted Jews. We have looked at some New Testament passages which lead to this conclusion. On the other hand we should also look at passages some have claimed demonstrate anti-Semitism in the New Testament.

Luke 13:6-9 gives us Jesus' parable of the barren fig tree. A man who owned a vineyard had a fig tree which did not yield fruit. He asked the gardener to cut it down but the gardener asked to give the tree more time and care and then to cut it down if it still remained barren. This parallels an account of Jesus cursing a fig tree which failed to bear fruit (Mark 11:12-14, 20-21). The fig tree did often represent Israel in biblical times so this was likely a prophecy of the destruction of the Jewish nation for their failure to live in righteousness before God.

In the context of other parables and teachings (see the parable of the wicked tenants below) it appears that it could also be speaking of the sin of the nation as a political entity, not the Jewish people as a whole, in their rejection of Jesus and his teachings. This would place guilt solely upon certain Jewish leaders as well as those who agreed with those leaders. This parable would not place guilt upon the Jewish people as a whole since we know that there were always a large number of Jewish followers of Jesus before his death as well into the centuries following (Matt 4:25; Acts 1:15; 2:41; 21:20).

Part II: Bad Religion?

Mark 12:1–12, the parable of the wicked tenants, is a story Jesus told about a vineyard owner who sends his servants to collect his portion of the crop but who are cast out by the tenant farmers. The servants represent prophets who are abused and sometimes killed by a people who should produce fruit, moral justice and righteousness, for the master and owner of the vineyard, God. Lastly the master sends his own son whom the workers kill. The son is Jesus and the tenant workers are the Jewish leaders and other Jewish people who reject Jesus and later kill him. The owner will then kill the tenant farmers and give the vineyard to others. This parable likely alludes to another parable mentioned in Isaiah 5:1–30 which predicted the destruction of the Jewish nation by the Babylonians. Jesus' parable thus possibly predicts the destruction of the Jewish nation, but it at least predicts a change in the vineyard and its workers. The evil tenants are gone and new workers who are worthy now bring forth the fruit of righteousness and moral goodness. We are not told that Gentiles are the new workers so the parable does fit the early development of the church which was made up of first Jewish and then Jewish and Gentiles believers. God's tenants are no longer merely the people of the Jewish nation, now they are all and only Jews and Gentiles who obey God.

This parable cannot be honestly read as promoting anti-Semitism. It is a condemnation of Jewish leaders as well as likely many other Jewish people at this time. One important point we need to realize is that Jesus' criticism of Jewish leaders, teachers, and others does not amount to anti-Semitism. Jeremiah condemned Jewish kings, prophets, priests, scribes, and other political and religious leaders as well as many common people. Was Jeremiah anti-Semitic? Were Moses and the other prophets anti-Semitic because they did the same? Of course not. Yet because Jesus and other New Testament writers, all of whom were Jews except one, condemned Jewish leaders and some other Jews, they are maligned as being anti-Semitic. The one Gentile writer, Luke, merely compiled information and statements from Jewish followers of Jesus. Jewish priests, kings, and common people all tried to kill Jeremiah as well (Jer 36:26; 38:4, 6). Some Jewish kings succeeded in killing some of the other prophets. Was this anti-Semitic? Obviously it was not. Yet because the Gospel writers said certain Jewish leaders asked for Jesus' death, this is considered anti-Semitic. How ridiculous.

Matthew says that at Jesus' trial "all of the people" asked that his blood, responsibility for his death, be upon them and their children (Matt 27:25). From the context, it is clear that this is merely speaking of a specific group of Jewish people, possibly a large number, who were standing before Pilate. Of course, more than one person could not have actually said this at once without the statement becoming indecipherable noise. So probably one person, possibly the high priest, said it and then a number of others chimed in with some sign or indication of agreement.

To read this as a binding curse on all Jews is to read into this text far more than it says. There were likely many Jews even among those who were present who never asked for Jesus' death or to be responsible for his death. The fact that the speaker and his supporters expressed the desire for the responsibility for Jesus' death to be on themselves and their children does not give us reason to believe such responsibility fell on anyone but the speakers. Their request gives no reason to believe a curse was placed on Jesus' followers, who were Jewish, or any other Jews who did not request his death. Neither would God have reason to recognize as binding a curse on any of these people's children.

Even when Jewish people and leaders are specifically condemned for being responsible for Jesus' death, it is always within the context of an understanding that Gentile people and leaders are equally responsible (e.g., Acts 2:23; 4:24–28; 3:13–15, 17).

In one of Paul's statements only Jewish antagonists are singled out for killing Jesus and persecuting his followers (1 Thess 2:14–16). Paul spoke this way because of the parallelism of his statement. He said that just as it is Gentiles who persecute Gentile Christians, so Jews persecute Jewish Christians and killed Jesus. To keep the parallelism Paul also omitted mention of Jews who persecuted Gentile Christians and Gentiles who persecuted Jewish Christian, which obviously occurred at this time but less often. Had Paul been asked to be more accurate and complete in his statement, he would have admitted this and he would have admitted that Gentile leaders were also responsible for Jesus' death. Paul certainly did not have some tradition which claimed that only Jews killed Jesus. There was no tradition at this time which claimed such a thing and all of the Gospels claim both Jewish and Gentile participation. Paul is obviously not saying that all Jews or even that only Jews are responsible for killing Jesus and persecuting Jewish Christians.

Jesus and the Jewish Christians all considered themselves to be Jewish. Look at what Paul says about himself as he almost boasts about his Jewishness in Romans 11:1. Paul is obviously assuming that only certain Jews had killed Jesus and persecuted Jewish Christians just as he assumes

Part II: Bad Religion?

that only certain Gentiles have persecuted Gentile Christians—and Paul is condemning both groups. There is clearly nothing in this statement which is anti-Semitic. There is nothing here that contradicts his other statements that God has not rejected the Jews, that all Jews are beloved of God for the sake of the patriarchs, or that all Jews will be grafted back into the trunk of God's redeemed people and be saved (Rom 11).

Some writers will see a progression of increasingly anti-Semitic views in the Gospels from earlier to later writings. It becomes pretty obvious to anyone listening to their arguments however that they have to cherry-pick verses to read anti-Semitism into the texts. This is nothing one would see in the texts unless one first assumed that it must be there. If the early church created the story of Jesus' trial and death and wanted to exonerate Pilate and deny Gentile participation, they could have done so much more easily by simply having Herod kill Jesus. But in fact, because we see both Jews and Gentiles as responsible for his death, we see that all people are responsible because they are represented by these two categories of people.

In fact, Jesus claimed that no one could take his life but that he willingly gave it up (John 10:17–18), certainly an unusual statement coming from the last written Gospel and the one which should be most anti-Semitic. The point of Jesus' statement is that it is the sins of all people which require Jesus' death if they are to be redeemed, yet it was Jesus' choice as to whether he would go through with the decision to bring about that redemption. No one forced Jesus to die and yet we all, Jews and Gentiles alike, are responsible for his death.

Jesus was the lamb who was slain from the foundation of the earth (Rev 13:8). The persons of the trinity all have the same will. Since the first events of creation which included Adam and Eve's first sin, Jesus, in one accord with the decision of God the Father, chose to go through with this act of self-sacrifice. When Jesus made this decision in 33 CE in a garden near Jerusalem, this was the same decision he had made at the beginning of earth's history. This decision was transposed from one point of time (or perhaps it was a timeless event in the mind of God) to another point in time just two thousand years ago. I bring up this scenario to point out that it is possible for Jesus to choose to go through with his execution and yet when he made this decision just before his capture, he could not have chosen then not to give up his life. Both decisions were the same decision, thus, in a way, the first determined what the second would be.

Is the New Testament Anti-Semitic?

John's Gospel was probably written after the destruction of Jerusalem for an exclusively or almost exclusively Gentile audience. The writer usually used the terms "the Jews" to refer to the Jewish inhabitants of Judea. He possibly used the term so that his readers would keep in mind that these were the primary people around at this time in Judea. He usually wanted to be clear when he was speaking of Jews as distinct from Gentiles. He used this term to indicate Jewish opponents of Jesus yet he also made it clear at times that many Jews believed in him and followed him (e.g., John 11:45; this is stated about seven times in John). John even spoke of some Jewish leaders who became his followers (John 3:1–2; 19:38–39; 12:42; see also Luke 23:50–51). So even when John speaks of "the Jews" being his enemies or calling for his death, it is clear that this is simply his shorthand way of saying a specific group of Jewish people who were Jesus' enemies. John was obviously not saying all Jews were his enemies.

I have claimed that *if* the entire New Testament spoke of no one other than Jewish people as being responsible for Jesus' death (it does not), this still would be no indication of anti-Semitism. It would be no more anti-Semitic than the fact that ancient Jewish kings long before the time of Jesus, and with strong popular support, also killed prophets and that those prophets condemned the evil actions of those kings. We are only concerned about whether the New Testament is in any way anti-Semitic. Whatever meaning people read into the scripture for whatever possible reasons they might have is of no concern to us. Clearly the New Testament is in no way anti-Semitic.

20

The Canaanite Conquest

PROBABLY THE MOST DIFFICULT problem for Jews and Christians who believe the God of the Hebrew Bible should be seen as a good and just God is the problem of the Canaanite conquest. The exodus was the migration of the tribes of Israel out of slavery from Egypt into Canaan. With the exception of certain specified nations, the biblical account tells us that God commanded the Israelites to destroy all of the inhabitants of the land they were entering including innocent children (Deut 20:16–18). Our problem is that it is difficult to imagine how the God of the Bible can be considered to be good who would command such slaughter.

Some would want to speak of this as a Canaanite genocide but I question whether this is the best way to describe these events. Many biblical scholars will claim that far fewer people were killed than a surface reading of the text might suggest. And I am told that to be able to speak of a *genocide* we need some pretty big numbers. So I will normally call it the Canaanite conquest.

I leave it to biblical scholars like Paul Copan to more exhaustively deal with the problems I will cover very quickly. Many of the points he makes I will not touch on at all. I would again suggest his book, *Is God a Moral Monster* as well as his more scholarly work with Matthew Flannagan, *Did God Really Command Genocide?* as the first places to look.

So how should we look at this problem? The first thing we should notice is that four hundred years before the conquest occurred God promised Abraham this land would be given to his descendants. It cannot be given to him now, God told Abraham, because the wickedness of the people was not yet great enough to warrant their destruction and displacement (Gen 15:13–14, 16). This was God's punishment of a very evil culture. There is some other historical evidence in addition to the claims in the Hebrew scripture that these societies practiced a very gruesome form of child sacrifice. The culture was so evil that it had to be destroyed or dispersed so that the social evils it had established, most notably child sacrifice, would end.

This would be my second point. The evils of these societies were so ingrained and institutionalized that the only way they could be eradicated was by a complete destruction or dispersion of the populations and thus a destruction of the culture.

William Lane Craig has been criticized for suggesting that the soldiers who killed the children would have been traumatized by what they did. If they were around today they would need therapy for post traumatic stress disorder. However, as a critic might object, after lopping off a child's head, it sounds a little silly to talk about feeling sorry for the soldier.

I think it would be better to avoid the *traumatized soldiers* claim and see that in fact killing these children probably did not bother the soldiers at all. This would be my third point. Most people of the time may have been what we might classify today as *semi-barbaric*. Perhaps the Israelites were as well. This does not mean that they were not far advanced in their ethics over many societies of the time. Just look at the ethics of the Mosaic law as compared to the laws of surrounding nations.[1] Or consider the high moral theology we find in the book of Job (e.g., chap. 31). Few people even today have been able to live up to the heights of this ethical ideal. Nevertheless, the invading Israelites may have been semi-barbaric in this regard: they may have had no qualm about killing a child or woman or anyone else regarded as an enemy. I should add that any suggestion that women could not be just as evil as men betrays a tacit sexism. Our discovery of unspeakable atrocities committed by women under Hitler's regime quickly erases this naive belief.

Because the soldiers were not aware of any evil they had done, they were not guilty of this evil any more than a lion would be guilty if it kills a child who wanders too far from its village. For God to use these soldiers to kill children was no different than had he sent a plague to do so. God would not have to command someone to act in opposition to their conscience. As I said earlier, I think that it is likely that this was a common moral condition

---

1. Copan makes this point quite often in *Is God a Moral Monster?* See also Walton, *Bible Background Commentary, Old Testament,* to look at specific laws in the Bible.

of the people at this time in history. It would take many prophets and finally the teachings of Jesus to overcome the ethical blindness of believing that there is no problem with the face to face killing of innocent children.

This brings us to my fourth point. We find in Jesus' teachings a very high value placed on children. He said that we must become like children in innocence to enter the kingdom of God. Children should not be hindered from being brought to him because, he said, of such are the kingdom of God. He said that what we do to the least—the most rejected, those of lowest social esteem, the most oppressed—we have done to him. In the parable of the sheep and the goats (Matt 25:31–46) he went on to say that what we do to him will determine whether we are accepted by God or face God's judgment in the life to come. When Jesus says "what you have done to the least of these," it is very difficult for one to come away feeling that he is not speaking of children, at the very least. He spoke about it being better to have a heavy millstone tied around one's neck and thrown into the sea than to cause a child who believes in him to sin. He said we need to be very careful not to despise or offend a child. Their angels are constantly standing before the face of God (Matt 18:1–6, 10). With these teachings no follower of Jesus could harm a child. This is something God could no longer ask of us after the time of Jesus.

The fifth point is that the people were given the opportunity to flee rather than be destroyed. One inhabitant of a city which was about to be destroyed said that they had heard of the miracles the Israelite God had done in overcoming the powerful Egyptian army. They knew the Israelites were on their way to Canaan and that no one else had been able to stand against them. Their hearts melted in fear as they knew the Israelites were getting nearer (Josh 2:8–11; Deut 2:25; Josh 9:24). And yet these people were also given plenty of time to leave this land; they had forty years with the full knowledge of what was coming. The few good people, not to mention many evil people, who lived in some of these evil nations could have left. I would suspect that many people did actually leave their homes to emigrate to other lands.

The sixth point is that the Bible tells us that for whatever undeserved suffering one endures, one receives equal or greater recompense or compensation. For example, Paul speaks of our state in heaven far outweighing any pain we endure in this life (Rom 8:18). Whether this means the children who were killed go directly to paradise or return to another life in this world or to another world much like this one, the end result is the same: the child is not to be pitied and can hardly be considered even a victim.

The Canaanite Conquest

Some children who were killed may of course have been old enough to have committed some evil deserving of some degree of judgment. Nevertheless, the point still remains that for any undeserved suffering they endure, God provides equal recompense for that suffering. Of course the fact that someone believes that God gives compensation for any such suffering does not give one the right to otherwise harm, much less kill, children. It is the other factors we have discussed which make the difference and, in this case specifically, would allow for the soldiers to kill children.

Sometimes it is assumed that the evil of killing a child is so absolute that there are categorically no conditions which will justify it. This is simply false. Even in modern warfare, no matter how humane it may attempt to be, some *collateral damage* will be inevitable. Arial bombing, artillery, and, more recently, missiles and drones will kill innocent children even when military leaders do their best to pinpoint only military targets. We usually see this as necessary at times to stop an enemy. So even today we recognize that killing innocent children is sometimes necessary to prevent a greater evil. Killing children is not such an absolute moral evil that it must be unconditionally avoided.

My seventh point concerns the kind of suffering the child endures. Some might ask whether killing children in a military conquest is morally different from killing children by child sacrifice. It definitely is. The institutionalized evil of child sacrifice will continue generation after generation. The killing of children in a military conquest will happen only once. Also, the kind of death is enormously different. Being burned to death alive is vastly different from the quick slash of a sword to the neck.

My eighth point is that God has the right to destroy anyone or everyone—whether innocent or guilty, good or evil—as God did with the great flood. It is God's right to take any life whenever God chooses. (The ostensive reason for the great flood was the wickedness of the people, Gen 6:5–7. Nevertheless, we must assume that the children killed were innocent.)

In fact, there are some skeptics who have argued that God does not have the right to take *any* life. If we were able to make a robot that feels pain and is conscious, we would not have the right to destroy it, would we? But this scenario is very different from the idea of divine creation. We come from God as our source. We are not a collection of parts God puts together which just happen by chance to be conscious and aware of pain. Our consciousness comes from God. God breathed into us the breath of life. As God gave us life, so God has the right to take it back. Assuming the biblical account of creation by God, our lives belong to God and God has the right to cause them to cease to exist if God so chooses and whenever God so chooses.

The only limit on God's choice to do with us as God desires is God's absolute goodness. If God allows us undeserved suffering, a greater good will result for us. However, if God is absolutely good, this intuitively counts against the possibility that God could cause anyone to cease to exist. Though we can imagine that God has the right to choose to annihilate any or all of us because God has created us, if God is absolutely good, it appears doubtful that God could ever do so. Also, a good case can be made that a better reading of the Bible would tell us that no one will ever cease to exist.

As far as the issue of the flood or the Canaanite conquest is concerned, the crucial point is that no matter how good or evil anyone is, God chooses and has the right to choose when any person will die though it is doubtful that anyone will completely cease to exist.

The ninth point would be that the child's death could be a punishment for the parents. If you know that not only are you going to die but also your children and that your entire posterity will cease, you will face much greater emotional distress. The loss of one's posterity, the discontinuation of one's name through one's descendants, was one of the greatest losses these people could imagine. One might think this seems a little odd to say given my claim that child sacrifice was one of the main reasons God wanted these societies destroyed. But child sacrifice did not destroy the entirety of one's line. So it may be that God wanted the evil Canaanites to know this particular kind of punishment, seeing their children killed and their linage end, as well as knowing they would die themselves.

Remember that the child loses nothing. Death for the child is just the transition from one good or bad state (however good or bad their lives may have been) to another state. Also, remember that any undeserved suffering for the child is at least exactly compensated.

In summary, we might see this explanation as follows. God took advantage of the Israelite's ethical partial-blindness, having them carry out actions they did not believe were wrong in order to have certain evil nations destroyed. God had judged that these nations were so evil they should be destroyed or dispersed. This would also be the best way God could eliminate the enormous social evil of child sacrifice. God did nothing morally wrong in commanding the killing of innocent children since God did not even face the moral difficulty of having the Israelites do something they believed was evil.

The Canaanite Conquest

I think this is intuitively one of the most crucial aspects of the problem we must deal with. We imagine God telling a soldier to kill an innocent child against the soldier's deep moral conviction not to do so. But if to the soldier such an act is no different than killing an adult enemy, then God's use of the soldier as a tool to kill the child is no different than God sending a plague to wipe out a town.

So (continuing the summary) imagine our situation: God wants a society of very evil people killed but is merciful enough to allow them to merely leave their countries. By fleeing, their numbers would be too small to culturally influence the nations they would be entering to reestablish the old institutionalized evils. God could have simply killed them directly as happened with the flood or at Sodom and Gomorrah. But if there were a group of people around who would be willing to kill them, who did not think it was evil to do so, and to whom God wanted to give this land, the displaced people would still have the opportunity to flee. Would it not then be more merciful for God to do this and to give the Israelites this land than for God to kill them directly?

Admittedly, there were some whom God did not allow to flee to surrounding countries. God hardened their hearts so that they would choose to fight the Israelites and thus be killed. These would then be like the people killed in the flood whom, except for the children, God had decided were so evil they should not live. Nevertheless, the biblical account of the conquest of Canaan indicates that there were many people who were very fearful of the Israelites and who could have emigrated to other lands as individuals and families.

It is important to remember that this is almost entirely a hypothetical problem. We are not concerned about whether the flood or the exodus or the conquest actually occurred. Some archeological and historical evidence does apply which gives some indication that horrific child sacrifices did occur in this area. But even if it did not, all that we are ultimately concerned about is what the Bible claimed occurred and possible scenarios concerning that account. We are concerned about the biblical statements that the Israelites should kill these people, that child sacrifice occurred, and that God considered these people to be so evil that some should be entirely destroyed and that some should be allowed to flee their countries rather than be killed. We are concerned about whether the God depicted in the Bible can be judged as evil or not. With the nine points we have covered, we see that this God cannot be accused of evil.

21

Can Child Molesters Go to Heaven?

SAM HARRIS LIKES TO mock the Christian view of redemption and reconciliation with God. He offers stories similar to the following: Imagine a child molester had raped and then buried his latest victim alive. He has been captured and tried and is now on his way to execution. He had just accepted Jesus as his savior, enjoyed his favorite meal, and with a painless lethal injection is awakened to eternal joy and bliss. But good Muslims, Jews, Buddhists, even good and caring atheists all have to go to eternal torment at death. Maybe even the little girl he had molested and killed will burn in hell because she wasn't old enough to become a Christian. Or so some evangelical Christians might believe. Some other Christians think that if she was not baptized she will be denied entrance to heaven. If such views are correct, would they not amount to a grave, indeed a horrific injustice, to say the least? Does the Bible teach such things and encourage injustice?

There are several problems with such views from a Christian perspective. We have discussed earlier how good Muslims, Jews, Buddhists, atheists, and any other non-Christians do not necessarily receive punishment in the coming age, so I won't repeat my arguments here. I will only say that what determines one's salvation or damnation is how one responds to God's Spirit who speaks to and draws all people even if they have never heard of Jesus.

I have also given arguments that though there may be some who are eternally condemned by God, nonetheless they will also be in some sense eventually accepted by God; a doctrine of eternal conscious torment for the lost is not at all the most likely biblical view. I have also argued that children who die prematurely, before they have the ability to make decisions which determine their relationship with God, will not face punishment in the next life. (My own view, which I have argued, was that they will be given another opportunity to live past moral maturity and to make those decisions which determine their relationship with God. They would be given the opportunity to live this long in another physical world like this one or in a spiritual world, or, possibly, they would even be allowed to return to a new life in this world.)

But what about our child molester? Does he get to go directly to heaven? First of all we need to recognize that there are biblical passages which indicate that some people, after resisting for so long God's Spirit drawing them to God, God will eventually give over to their desires and false beliefs and no longer call them to himself (Rom 1:21–25; 2 Thess 2:9–12). No one can come to God or be accepted by God unless God first draws them (John 6:44), which, I have argued, God does for all people. Some have in this life passed beyond the possibility of salvation because God will no longer call them to himself.

So it is not the case that someone like Hitler or this child molester can necessarily be accepted by God if they just happen to repent. It may be that they must remain lost if they have consistently resisted God in the past. Only God determines how long that resistance might be for each individual before they cross the line of reprobation. They may be unable to repent because God no longer allows them the ability to repent or God simply refuses to hear them.

Secondly, we need to better understand the biblical notion of God's justice as it applies to those who are not lost. We cannot do evil thinking we can avoid the consequent punishment simply because we know that God will forgive. Possibly God will forgive, but that does not mean one will not face punishment. David committed murder and adultery, possibly even rape, and, when confronted with his sin, repented and was forgiven. But when the prophet told him he was forgiven he also told David he would have to face punishment (2 Sam 11, 12:1–14). God's forgiveness only kept him from immediate death. If the child molester thought he could get away with his crime by eventually asking God's forgiveness, and if he was not beyond forgiveness, God would possibly have treated him as he treated David. So depending on his earlier resistance to God, it may be that God would not forgive him at all or it may be that God would forgive but also require pain and punishment. Some sins are so grievous that it is difficult to imagine that God will not require some greater punishment even if the individual is forgiven. But God alone knows the person's present and previous inmost thoughts and intentions. God knows if or how much the child molester acted out of ignorance (which is hard to imagine) and how much out of willful wickedness.

At this point we can only say that God will be just. Abraham asked (rhetorically), "Will not the judge of all the earth do right?" (Gen 18:25). We have seen God's dealing with David's willful evil was just and right in a way it likely could never have been had we been David's judge. Whatever the outcome, God will be just.

There are clear instances in the New Testament of punishment and warning to Christians who sin that judgment will come to them even though they are still fully accepted by God. Some believers who partook of the communion meal without honoring it as representative of Christ's body became ill and some died prematurely (1 Cor 11:27–32); Peter said that judgment begins in the house of God (1 Pet 4:17); God chastens those he loves (Heb 12:5–11); and Paul, speaking to Christians, said that they will reap what they sow (Gal 6:7).

For those Christians whom God has determined require such chastening but who die before receiving it, God would have to allow them a time of punishment after death before being accepted into God's presence. Catholics believe in such a time of purgatory for some Christians. From the passages we have looked at, this outcome appears to be the only feasible alternative for some individuals. So we see that the child molester, if he is accepted by God after having repented, may not be immediately received into paradise at death but may endure a time of punishment first. All in all, though Harris's complaint might be accepted under a certain popular Christian understanding, a complete biblical understanding does not allow for the injustice he imagines.

We have been able to dispose of some questionable Christian teachings which paint the biblical God as evil. We have looked at enough morally problematic passages in the Bible to see that there are likely good explanations for any others we might come up with and that they do not malign the goodness of the biblical God. My claim is that the God described in the Bible can only be good and that Christian teaching will produce more good in the world than evil.

22

Atheism's Moral Problem

AFTER HAVING LOOKED AT religious and secular institutions and belief systems I have offered the conclusion that religion cannot be shown to produce more harm than secular beliefs or institutions. I have also claimed that many of the evils ascribed to Christianity or to Christian scripture can be demonstrated to produce less harm than good or, in many cases, to produce much good and no harm at all. At this point it would be good to shift our investigation and look at some basic moral problems with atheism.

Christians and other theists sometimes present an argument which claims that unless a good God exists, we have no grounds for claiming that any actions are objectively morally good or evil. This argument says that since we do know that some actions are objectively morally wrong, that since this belief is not just our subjective impression, it would follow that God must exist. Let's assume, just for the sake of the argument, that this moral argument *fails* and atheists can consistently affirm that some things are simply and truly objectively right and wrong given their world view. (For the time being I will leave it to others to defend this moral argument.)

Next we need to consider something we may call *Ivan's dictum*. At one point in his novel, *The Brothers Karamazov*, Dostoyesky has the brothers Ivan and Alyosha in a conversation. Ivan claims that if there is no immortality, then all things are lawful. If this is our only life, Ivan's dictum would say, then there are no binding rules. Once you are dead, you are nothing and nothing matters. Now Western atheism usually does assume that this is our only life. So without looking at some of the more extraneous forms of atheism we might explore, for now we should assume that this is the kind of atheism we are concerned about and that under atheism death is the end of our existence.

When atheists say this is our only life but we still need to avoid evil and to help the hurting just because they are suffering and when they say that some wrongs are truly and undeniably evil, other atheists, maybe a Stalin or Mao, may be quite tempted to say, "So what? So what if it really is evil to throw a four year old into a blazing furnace? You tell me, 'It's objectively, morally wrong!' Okay, I got that. So what does that matter? If this is my only life and the four year old's only life, why should I be concerned about anything I do so long as I'm pretty sure I can get away with it?"

Richard Wurmbrand was an underground Christian leader in Communist Romania who spent years imprisoned for his faith. One of his torturers told him that he thanked God, in whom he did not believe, that he could live at a time when he could express all of the evil in his heart—what he did and what he loved doing more than anything else was inflicting pain, it was torturing people. There is no afterlife. There will be no judgment, no heaven or hell. So what does it matter what evil one does? Sure it matters to the one suffering. But what can you say to the one causing the suffering? You cannot just say that it's objectively morally wrong to do that. He or she will just tell you, "So what?"

Sometimes our courts run into true psychopaths. Have you ever heard people interviewed who will tell the most horrible things they have done; people who have absolutely no sense of moral guilt, no sense of good or evil, just a sense of, What can I do to get away with this? Their minds are totally pragmatically oriented. They sleep peacefully at night. They do not believe in a God who will judge them and punish them in the next life. There is no next life. And what they would say to any atheist who questions their behavior would be the same thing: "This is my only life. This is your only life. Soon you and I will not be and soon all those I've hurt or killed or tortured will not be. We're all ultimately nothing anyway."

Victor Stenger was a scientist who wrote several books arguing for atheism. He did not take the kind of amoralist position I am describing here, but as an atheist he has made statements which lead to that view. At a conference for atheists his closing words were "We're all just frozen nothings."[1] The amoralist will say, "How can you even hurt a nothing? So what does it matter what I've done and what does it matter what you do?"

---

1. Stenger, "Origins," *Skeptics Society Conference*.

Atheism's Moral Problem

I do not think the morally oriented atheist has anything to say to the psychopathic amoralist.

Plato in the *Republic* has Socrates consider the story of Gyges's magic ring. With this ring he can make himself invisible and do any evil he wishes. No one can stop him or threaten him with punishment in this life and they do not consider the possibility of judgment in the next life. Why should he not do whatever he wishes? Plato never adequately answers this question.

What may be the more prudential choice for you, what may benefit you more, is often not the best moral choice. And when it is a choice between the two, between the moral and the prudential when they conflict, unless one has a distinct motivation to choose the moral, one will choose the prudential. There is nothing intrinsic to atheism that will motivate one to choose the moral over what is more prudentially beneficial to oneself.

We might even be able to make this amoralist justification sound not quite so morally repugnant. Suppose for whatever reason—money, power, revenge, or whatever—someone wants to take another person's life. Couldn't we imagine them asking something like the following: "If everyone has to die sooner or later, what difference does it make if it's just a little sooner for some? When they're dead, they're gone forever anyway. Everyone will be nothing eventually. How can just a few years make any difference for those who are ultimately nothing anyway?"

If you have not seen it, watch the Woody Allen movie, *Crimes and Misdemeanors*. A man has a mistress who threatens to tell his wife of their affair and destroy his marriage and family. He hires a hit man and has her killed. He worries about whether he may get caught and ponders what he has done and should do. Then it turns out someone else gets charged for the crime and the family never finds out anything about the affair. It's as if nothing had ever happened. The murderer can walk away saying, "What a wonderful world we live in."

Now many people might want to say, "Well, I know some things are just wrong and that gives me the motivation to never do something like that. I could never take another person's life no matter what my motivation might be." Now I honestly would hope people would say something like that. I would hope everyone would say that. The problem is, if you are an atheist, I don't think you would have anything to say to the atheist who wants to do such a thing. It is entirely up to the individual, it's up to their choice, whether they live a moral life or whether they choose to make their own morality and live a life that is more prudential to their own perceived well-being—which may just involve harm to someone else.

Proper education will not solve this problem or bring about a moral society. One cannot just instruct Gyges that he should follow his moral motivation, his sense that he ought to do what is good and right, that he should not kill the king or rape the queen or take their wealth or kingdom. Here we need to simply think about the reasons people choose to do good or evil when there is no ostensive religious motivation.

What could give someone a motivation to avoid wrongly harming someone one wants to harm? One would need to be lucky enough to have something in one's social environment or one's upbringing that will strongly motivate them not to do so. Of course, one's moral sense itself might provide motivation. But unless one clings to that moral sense, just about the only way they will keep it is if they happen to have strong social ties that motivate them to do so. And there have been cultures in which the social controls have been strong enough to generally produce moral societies without the presence of religious motivations.

Confucianism, for example, though it has been criticized for its non-egalitarian, misogynous, and excessively ritualistic features, displays a very beautiful ethical core. Historically it has become strongly engrained in the ethos of a number of Eastern nations and it has helped to produce solidly ethical societies without relying on transcendent religious motivations.

So it can be done. But notice the problems we now face. One has to be lucky enough to have been raised in such a strongly socially controlling society to have that kind of strong motivation to live morally. More importantly, one does not thereby have good reason for living morally, one simply does so because of those strong social attachments. One may so strongly value the opinion of, say, the father of the family that one would willingly give up one's life rather than to have his disapproval. The Japanese willingness to give up one's life for the Fatherland by suicide in the Second World War shows to what harmful and bizarre extremes such devotion will lead. In any case, for a secular morality to work in a society, it is important to have strong social networks and a strong commitment to the social bonds within those networks.

If we happen to be brought up in the wrong kind of home or environment, one without strong internal social ties or one with strong ties but bad moral ideals, or if we let ourselves be influenced by the wrong kind of friends or authority figures, if we do not let that moral awareness motivate us, we probably will not continue to cling to that moral awareness. So for the most part we just have to be *lucky* as to what social environment we are born into and grow up in and live in. Or we have to just happen to choose to cling to our natural moral awareness in spite of our environment in order to be ethically responsible atheists.

But worse, because we are a thinking beings, we may end up like Nietzsche and reject our moral awareness and moral upbringing and moral environment. We may conclude, like Ivan, that because there is no immortality, then all things are lawful and acceptable.

The big problem with atheism then is that there is no sufficiently motivating ethic which is intrinsic to atheism as such. Atheists may be very moral people, if they happen to choose that, or they may be very immoral. It's all up to one's choice. One may choose to be a Mother Theresa or one may choose to be an Adolf Hitler. There is nothing intrinsic to atheism that will motivate a person one way rather than the other. These are some of the basic ethical problems with atheism.

On the other hand, in a high ethical religion like Christianity one has a strong motivation to accept and follow the moral law one is aware of by nature, one's obligation to do good to others and not to harm them. One is motivated out of love for God. The Christian is motivated to obey God because they believe God chose to incarnate and endure an unimaginably painful death as a sacrifice since this was the only way God could bring us reconciliation with God. The Christian is also motivated out of fear of God. We should indeed fear facing God's judgment if we have knowingly caused someone's undeserved harm. If there is a creator and if all of existence is as it should be, then God must be absolutely just. If we cause someone undeserved harm and God judges us, we are getting what we deserve.

Good without God?

Some would claim that it is more noble to help others simply out of concern for their suffering than because someone thinks God has asked them to do so. But if the reason God asks someone is because God wants them to begin to make the choice to help others just out of concern for their suffering, then this is no less noble. In this view God wants them to see others as valuable just because of what they are, as conscious beings who experience pain. And because they have value, God also sees them as valuable. But of course, in this view it is God who created them as they are, and because of

Part II: Bad Religion?

what they are, conscious beings, they have value. This religious motivation is not a bad reason for helping others. It is rather the secularist ethic which cannot sustain a good reason for helping others.

The deeper problem for the atheist is that they cannot justify this notion of nobility to which they seek to appeal. Is it more noble to do good for its own sake as Sam Harris says? In fact, it is not. Being "good for goodness sake" becomes as silly and shallow as it sounds. When he talks of helping the hurting "purely out of concern for their suffering" then we may more readily agree.[2] But even here we may question just how *noble* such a notion really is or what an appropriate motivation might be to do this.

Why are we motivated to be concerned to help the hurting just because they are hurting? Is it merely because this motivation, this sense of compassion, has somehow been programmed into our brains through our evolutionary history? Do we think this way because it has some survival advantage? Maybe if the group survives, the individual has a better chance of surviving. But often this motivation is in conflict with more competitive motivations. Our "selfish gene" will often cause us to seek to destroy, not care for others since anyone else could be a competitor. When such motivations conflict, do we have good reason to affirm one over the other?

If the motivation of helping the hurting simply because they are hurting is more than merely an artifact of our evolutionary history, if there is something transcendent about the human awareness of good and evil, something that comes from a divine source, then we may have reason to seek to follow its leading. Otherwise, we are merely obeying our brains which just happen to have been programmed to think this way. If we happen to be programmed to have compassion on the hurting, is that good reason to do so? Is the sense of nobility Harris appeals to nothing more than a feeling produced when the body releases certain chemicals to certain parts of the brain?

If one still wishes to affirm and appeal to the nobility of moral compassion, one faces other problems. When Nietzsche says it is more noble to stand aloof of traditional ideals of goodness and care for others, that it is in fact noble to avoid moral restraint, "a device created by religion to contravene the natural order of dominance of the strong over the weak," he promotes a competing view of nobility which many find more appealing.[3] Antitheists like Harris may laud the nobility of helping others "purely out of

---

2. Harris, *Letter to a Christian Nation*, 34.
3. Abelson, "History of Ethics," 98.

concern for their suffering" but they cannot refute those like Nietzsche who think nobility has more to do with domination and with standing strong with no concern for others. The appeal to nobility may lead one in a direction very different from that which Harris espouses.

For the secularist who sees the horrible end of Nietzsche's nobility and cannot embrace it, there still remains a deep nihilism which darkens Harris's glowing and optimistic motivation to moral good. Ivan's dictum still negates his appeal to nobility for moral hope. As much as we might hope that our moral sensitivity to the needs of others will motivate us to concern and care for the suffering, the dark night of death and annihilation often crushes all such hope. Moral despair too often simply says, "If soon they will be nothing then they (and we) are all ultimately nothing anyway. Why should we be concerned about the hurting? Why should we even bother?"

When it is easy and convenient, then, yes, we may help someone purely out of concern for their suffering. Our conscience alone may motivate us to do so. But will we do it when it would cost us to do so? Will we do so when a crowd surrounds and taunts and tortures a single helpless person, when we may even lose our own lives should intervene? Remember that this is what happened fairly often not too long ago in Hitler's empire. But again, even when it is easy and convenient to help the hurting, our awareness of our nothingness, that soon we will cease to be (and that those who are hurting will cease to be), often reduces all motivation for concern and involvement to unconcern.

Secularists sometimes talk about how the knowledge that life is limited and soon will end leads them to value each fleeting joy and pleasure and glimpse of beauty more than they ever could if they thought they would live forever. When they talk this way I have a very hard time taking them seriously. An animal which is not aware of the future may enjoy and value each passing moment if it could think, but should a human who is aware of the future? There can be no joy in each fleeting moment for those who are not out to completely deceive themselves. Anyone who will open their eyes will see that they are nothing and there *is* no "fleeting moment" of pleasure to cling to. I mentioned earlier that the late Victor Stenger said we are all just frozen nothings, a momentary existence of consciousness that comes to be and passes away. If he was right, *he* is now completely nothing. Where is that fleeting moment of beauty and enjoyment now, that momentary pleasure that he once hoped to cling to? And someone would seriously think that a momentary pleasure is something worth living for?

Part II: Bad Religion?

Stephen Hawking said that religion is for people who are afraid of the night. Dylan Thomas begged his dying father to go not "gentle into that good night."[4] He was right that one should not go easy into the secularist's night of death but only because it is *not* a good night. Some have even professed to believe that an afterlife of eternal conscious torment, the hell some Christians and Muslims believe in, would be better than the secularist hell of nothingness. Hawking *should* be afraid of the night. Only an animal mind which is unaware of the coming nothingness should be unafraid of that night. The cold, bleak night of nothingness will drive the honest to despair, but it will also, for all practical purposes, drive the morally conscious to moral nihilism, to moral unconcern and indifference.

Secular moralists, those Nietzsche called the flatheads, will rise up appalled at such defeat and despair but will be unable to avoid this conclusion. Grimacing to close tight their eyes against the light and hold their ears closed and secure against all reason, their voices cry out loud and shrill: "WE-*CAN*-BE-GOOD-WITHOUT-GOD!" But then once more the ghost of Nietzsche will rise and laugh the flatheads to scorn as he did so long ago. Yes, they may be good without God, but once they have no more battles to fight with religion to try to prove their point and once they see their own bleak and hopeless end, they will again choose the prudential over the moral. If they believe atheism is true, they have no reason to do otherwise.

But even more frightening, if we truly believe ourselves to be Stenger's frozen nothings, if that nothingness is our clearest and most honest nature, why not choose any life focus or goal, any ethic or any ethic substitute which happens to lift us from our moribund despair? If murdering Jews at Treblinka or Tutsi in Rwanda can provide any sense of excitement or diversion or life-goal dedication to make us forget who we are, what can anyone say to refrain those who so choose?

---

4. Part of the title of one of his more popular poems. Jones, *Poems of Dylan Thomas*, 239.

23

Summary

WE HAVE LOOKED AT religious and secular organizations, institutions, and belief systems and we have seen that generally evil cannot be shown to proceed from the religious more often than from the secular. The ethical content of secular and religious systems affects the amount of good or evil which proceeds from either. The degree of commitment the followers of such systems possess and express is also a strong contributing factor. Very strong commitment will cause one to be more likely to defend or advance a system by any means available, including sometimes harmful or evil means. But stronger commitment to highly moral teachings will also produce more good. When there are strong social and political pressures to wrongly do harm to others, just about the only power which will allow one to stand against such pressures is one's commitment to one's moral beliefs.

Any of the notorious evils ascribed to religions have been evident in secular institutions and ideologies as well. Corrupt leaders will produce great evil in both religious and secular organizations. We cannot say that the harm that has resulted from corrupt Christian leaders and a perverted form of Christianity (one allowing the Inquisition, witch hunts, pograms, etc.) would have never existed in some secular form had Christianity never existed. Also, a religion cannot be considered to be evil simply because it has evil leaders—at least so long as that religion officially renounces those evils.

Christianity among the world religions provides a uniquely strong motivation to attract followers and for followers to adhere to its high moral teachings. We have seen this through several examples. Christians have

Part II: Bad Religion?

cared for the outcasts and oppressed because Jesus said that what they do to them they have done to him (e.g., Peter Claver, Elizabeth of Hungary). Out of their dedication to Jesus, they endured the greatest suffering to defend or protect others (Father Kolbe, the ten Booms). These are examples of moral courage and sacrifice to which atheists would be far less likely to commit themselves. Christians have fought for reform and brought about renewal in depressed and dysfunctional societies (the Catholic Church among the nineteenth-century American Irish). Moral change occurred in individuals who embraced Christianity which would not likely have occurred without that religious change (the Strobels). Political systems which oppress and murder the innocent can be very attractive to some people given the right social pressures. Many have found in Christ reason and motivation to resist and flee such systems. Many would never have committed themselves to such systems had they known about and embraced Christianity (Hang Pin).

Several reasons can be offered for the church's survival and flourishing in its first centuries when constantly recurring persecutions should have wiped it out. Likely the major and simplest reason can be found in its practice of doing good to others: feeding the hungry, caring for the outcasts, nursing the sick, and often risking one's life to do so.

I have argued that the Bible indicates that monogamous same gender sex by constitutionally same sex attracted individuals is not condemned under a thoroughly biblical view; neither is transgender sexual identification. Christians sometimes condemn behavior considered harmless by non-Christians. Even the claims of those who condemn all same gender sexual relations, like anyone else's, need to be taken seriously and evaluated honestly. One's views should not be rejected simply because they oppose current popular opinion.

Religions do not promote superstition and irrational beliefs more than secular beliefs. Superstition can only be eliminated when both religious and secular beliefs are rationally assessed.

Several accounts and commands in the Bible appear to promote undue harm to others. Jesus suggested that sometimes God allowed such laws in the Hebrew scripture because of the hardness of the people's hearts, because they were not willing to accept better laws. Some of these laws changed under Jesus' teachings. Yet having these less optimal, lesser-of-two-evils laws was better than having none at all. We have looked at several such laws such as those concerning apparent forced marriage for rape victims and the law of warfare.

Summary

Jesus' teaching concerning divorce does not promote abusive relationships but encourages lifelong marital commitment and stability. Paul's teaching that man is the head of woman speaks of woman originating from man, not being in submission to him. Paul's command that women should be silent in the church likely applied only for special reasons and at special times in the early church. This and his teaching that women should not teach or have authority over men does not apply to all churches at all times. Women were undeniably involved in other vocal ministries in the church (prayer, prophecy, singing, etc.). Paul's teaching that women should submit to their husbands should be understood as a mutual submission of one to the other. The Genesis curse that a woman's husband would rule over her is done away with in Christ. There is neither male not female, slave nor free, Greek nor Jew, but all are one in Christ. In the early church women were deacons and leading officers in the church, one was even called an apostle.

Women had far less rights than men in Greek, Roman, and even Jewish cultures at the time of Jesus. This changed dramatically for Christians. It also changed after the time of Constantine when the empire officially tolerated Christianity and many old oppressive laws were repealed. The Indian custom of burning widows on their husbands' funeral pyres, and the painful practice of female circumcision and Chinese foot binding were outlawed or resisted through Christian influence.

Though some aspects of the laws concerning slavery in ancient Israel were allowed because of the hardness of the people's hearts, generally slaves were to be seen as little different than normal hired workers. Israelite slaves were freed after six years and sometimes less. With the coming of Jesus' teachings slavery was completely done away with. His teachings are incompatible with slavery.

It is a complete myth to see the New Testament as in any way anti-Semitic just as it is absurd to think of the Hebrew prophets as anti-Semitic because they condemned and were condemned by Jewish leaders and other Jewish people.

The God of the Hebrew scripture has sometimes been judged to be evil because of his command to destroy the Canaanite population, children and adults alike. But these were people whom God refrained from having destroyed until their wickedness was so great that justice required that it be done. Their practice of child sacrifice was so engrained that it required the entire destruction or dispersal of these nations. The Israelite soldiers were, like so many people of this time, semi-barbaric in the sense of having

Part II: Bad Religion?

no sense of wrong in killing an enemy's children. Thus God did not even face the moral difficulty of having the Israelites do something they believed was evil. With Jesus' teaching regarding children, God would never again ask someone to kill an innocent child in this way. Most of these conquered people had strong motivation and ample opportunity to flee before being attacked by the Israelites and many likely did so. Any innocent children who were killed, like any other innocent people, after death would receive from God complete recompense for any undeserved suffering they endured. If the God of the Bible exists and is just, this is what he would do. Their deaths were far less painful than anything they would have endured had they died by child sacrifice. Their deaths were also a part of the punishment of their evil parents. Perhaps more importantly than anything else, we need to remember that God has the right to take any life at any time God chooses. Some actions which would be evil for a person to do by their own decision, like taking a human life, cannot be evil for God to do.

By allowing the Canaanites the opportunity to escape before allowing Israel to destroy them, God was much more merciful to them than had he destroyed these people directly himself.

A common view of Christianity is that a very evil person like a child molester and murderer goes directly to paradise at death with no punishment whatsoever if they simply repent and have faith in Christ. The scripture rather indicates that often severe punishment is still required for someone like this even if they are accepted by God. In some cases a person will have so long resisted God that eventually God will no longer allow them the opportunity to choose reconciliation with God. In all cases, God will be just.

Atheists face a very serious moral problem. Even if they accept that some actions are objectively morally wrong, they cannot get around Ivan's dictum that if there is no God and immortality, then all things are lawful. If this is your only life, then it does not matter what you do even if you admit it is objectively morally wrong. Soon neither you nor your victim will exist, so how can it matter what is done to that victim, however horrible it may be?

Some may be lucky enough to have something in their social environment which will bring them to act and live according to their natural moral awareness—maybe their attachment or esteem for a very moral friend or parent. But in the long run if a secular person lacks that social environment, whether or not they will live morally depends upon their free

Summary

choice—and ultimately a very arbitrary choice at that—unless they happen to have stronger motivation to disregard their moral standards. In contrast, Christianity provides a very strong motivation for living up to a very high ethical standard.

Religions cannot be shown to produce more evil than good than secular belief systems since both may have good or evil ethical foundations and there are no other factors unique to religion as such which make a significant difference. But a deeply biblical Christianity, because of its moral foundation and its power to attract, capture, and retain followers deeply motivated to follow its teachings, definitely does produce more good than evil.

The most important biblical answers to the Problem of Evil tell us that God needs to know how we will respond to God in the face of suffering and how we will respond to others when we witness their suffering. Such testing is necessary since it is the only way for us to become something as great and good as God wants us to be. A good case can be made that not only does Christianity produce much good in the world but any suffering it requires is strongly outweighed by a greater good it produces. Racism, classism, sexism, oppression, slavery—all would cease if everyone would affirm and consistently follow Jesus' teachings. Christianity also strongly attracts and motivates followers to adhere to this high ethical standard. On the other hand, atheism can promise no motivation to deter a Hitler or a Stalin, a Manson or a Dahmer, from committing as much harm as the world would allow them to carry out.

Bibliography

Abelson, Raziel. "History of Ethics." *Encyclopedia of Philosophy*. 3 (1967) 81–100.
American College of Pediatricians. A position statement: "Gender Ideology Harms Children." http://www.acpeds.org/the-college-speaks/position-statements/gender-ideology-harms-children (accessed July 2017).
Bartchy, S. S. "Slavery." *International Standard Bible Encyclopedia*. 4 (1988) 539–46.
Beilby, James K., and Paul R. Eddy, eds., *Divine Foreknowledge: Four Views*. Downer's Grove, IL: Inter Varsity, 2001.
Bizot, Francois. "My Savior, Their Killer." *The New York Times*, 17 February 2009.
Boswell, John. *Christianity, Social Tolerance, and Homosexuality*. University of Chicago Press, 1980.
Brauch, Manfred. *The Hard Sayings of Paul*. Downers Grove, IL: InterVarsity, 1989.
Bruce, F. F. *The Hard Sayings of Jesus*. Downers Grove, IL: InterVarsity, 1983.
Burrell, David B., with A. H. Jones. *Deconstructing Theodicy: Why Job Has Nothing to Say to the Puzzle of Suffering*. Grand Rapids, MI: Brazos, 2008.
Carroll, Vincent, and David Shiflett. *Christianity on Trial: Arguments Against Antireligious Bigotry*. San Francisco: Encounter, 2002.
Colson, Charles, with Ellen Santilli Vaughn. *The Body: Being Light in the Darkness*. Dallas: Word, 1992.
Copan, Paul. *Is God a Moral Monster? Making Sense of the Old Testament God*. Grand Rapids, MI: Baker, 2011.
Copan, Paul, and Matthew Flannagan. *Did God Really Command Genocide?: Coming to Terms with the Justice of God*. Grand Rapids, MI: Baker, 2014.
Cowles, C. S., Eugene H. Merrill, Daniel L. Gard, and Tremper Longman III. *Show Them No Mercy: 4 Views on God and Canaanite Genocide*. Grand Rapids, MI: Zondervan, 2003.
Craig, William Lane. *On Guard for Students: A Thinker's Guide to the Christian Faith*. Colorado Springs, CO: David C. Cook, 2015.
Craig, William Lane vs. Sean Carroll. "God and Cosmology: The Existence of God in Light of Contemporary Cosmology." *Greer Heard Forum*. New Orleans, LA: New Orleans Baptist Theological Seminary, 21 February 2014. http://www.reasonablefaith.org/god-and-cosmology-the-existence-of-god-in-light-of-contemporary-cosmology (accessed January 2016).
Craig, William Lane vs. Sam Harris. "Is the Foundation of Morality Natural or Supernatural?" Notre Dame, IN: University of Notre Dame, April 2011. http://www.

Bibliography

reasonablefaith.org/is-the-foundation-of-morality-natural-or-supernatural-the-craig-harris#section_4 (accessed January 2017).

Craig, William Lane, and J. P. Moreland, eds. *The Blackwell Companion to Natural Theology*. Malden, MA: Wiley-Blackwell, 2009.

Craig, William Lane, and Walter Sinnott-Armstrong. *God? A Debate Between a Christian and an Atheist*. New York: Oxford University Press, 2004.

D'Souza, Dinesh. *What's So Great About Christianity*. Carol Stream, IL: Tyndale House, 2007.

Dawkins, Richard. *The God Delusion*. New York: Houghton Mifflin, 2006.

Ehrman, Bart. *God's Problem: How the Bible Fails to Answer Our Most Important Question—Why We Suffer*. New York: Harper Collins, 2008.

Ellsberg, Robert, ed. *By Little and By Little: The Selected Writings of Dorothy Day*. New York: Alfred A. Knopf, 1983.

Gaeddert, Beth. "Buddhist Leader Spurs Flap Over Style of Living." *Rocky Mountain News* (Denver, CO), 15 July 1980.

———. "Tibetan Buddhism Alive, Well in Boulder." *Rocky Mountain News* (Denver, CO), 14 July 1980.

Gagnon, Robert. *The Bible and Homosexual Practice: Texts and Hermaneutics*. Nashville: Abingdon, 2001.

Goebbels, Joseph. Diary entry in *Die Tagebücher von Joseph Goebbels*. Edited by Elke Fröhlich. Part I, *Aufzeichnungen 1923–1941*. Vol. 7, *Juli 1939–Marz 1940*. Munich: K. G. Saur, 1998.

Goetz, Stewart. "The Argument from Evil." In Craig and Moreland, *Natural Theology*, 449–97.

Habermas, Gary, and Michael Licona. *The Case for the Resurrection of Jesus*. Grand Rapids, MI: Kregel, 2004.

Harris, Sam. *Letter to a Christian Nation*. New York: Vintage, 2008.

Hasker, William. "An Open Theist Theodicy of Natural Evil." In Perszyk, *Molinism*. 281–302.

Hays, Richard. "Relations Natural and Unnatural: A Response to John Boswell's Exegesis of Romans 1." *Journal of Religious Ethics* 14 (1986) 184–215.

Hoehner, Harold. *Chronological Aspects of the Life of Christ*. Grand Rapids, MI: Zondervan, 1977.

Holland, Tom. "Why I Was Wrong About Christianity." *New Statesman*, 14 September 2016. http://www.newstatesman.com/politics/religion/2016/09/tom-holland-why-i-was-wrong-about-christianity (accessed August 2017).

Howard-Snyder, Daniel, ed. *The Evidential Argument from Evil*. Bloomington, IN: Indiana University Press, 1996.

Hurtado, Larry W. *Destroyer of the gods: Early Christian Distinctiveness in the Roman World*. Waco, TX: Baylor University Press, 2016.

Iannoccone, Laurence. "Introduction to the Economics of Religion." *Journal of Economic Literature* 36, no. 3 (September 1998) 1465–95. https://edisciplinas.usp.br/pluginfile.php/262957/mod_resource/content/2/Iannaccone%20-%20Economics%20of%20Religion.pdf (accessed October 2017).

Instone-Brewer, David. *The Jesus Scandals: Why He Shocked His Contemporaries (and Still Shocks Today)*. Oxford: Monarch, 2012.

"Jeffrey Dahmer." Wikipedia. https://en.wikipedia.org/wiki/Jeffrey_Dahmer (accessed November 2017)

Bibliography

Jensen, Dennis. "Einstein's Religion: Why Have the Greatest Scientists Believed in God?" http://www.encounter1.org/10-1/ (accessed September 2017).

———. *Flirting with Universalism: Resolving the Problem of an Eternal Hell.* Eugene, OR: Resource, 2014.

———."God's Foreknowledge and Human Suffering," http//www.encounter1.org/12-1/ (accessed October 2017).

———. "The Time of Messiah: Daniel's Prophecy of the Seventy Weeks." http://www.encounter1.org/3-1/ (accessed July 2017).

Jones, Clay. *Why Does God Allow Evil?: Compelling Answers for Life's Toughest Questions.* Eugene, OR: Harvest House, 2017.

Jones, Daniel, ed. *The Poems of Dylan Thomas.* New York: New Directions, 2003.

Keener, Craig. *The IVP Bible Background Commentary: New Testament.* Downers Grove, IL: InterVarsity, 1993.

Lewis, C. S. *The Great Divorce.* New York: Harper Collins, 1946.

———. *The Problem of Pain.* New York: MacMillan, 1962.

———. "On Obstinacy in Belief." Chap. 2 in *The World's Last Night and Other Essays.* New York: Harcourt Brace Jovanovich, 1960.

Lilienfeld, Scott O., and Rachel Ammirati. "Would the World Be Better Off Without Religion?" *Skeptical Inquirer* 38, no. 4 (July/August 2014). http://www.csicop.org/si/show/would_the_world_be_better_off_without_religion_a_skeptics_guide_to_the_deba/ (accessed January 2017).

MacGregor, Kirk R. "The Existence and Irrelevance of Gratuitous Evil." *Philosophia Christi* 14, no. 1 (2012) 168–80.

Marin, Peter. "Spiritual Obedience." *Harper's Magazine*, February 1979.

Martin, David. *Does Christianity Cause War?* Oxford: Oxford University Press, 1997.

Milgram, Stanley. "Behavioral Study of Obedience." *Journal of Abnormal and Social Psychology* 67, no. 4 (1963) 371–78.

Morris, Leon. *The New International Commentary on the New Testament: The Gospel According to John.* Revised Edition. Edited by Gordon D. Fee. Grand Rapids, MI: Eerdmans, 1995.

Murray, Charles. *Coming Apart: The State of White America, 1960–2010.* New York: Crown Forum, 2012.

O'Malley, William J. "The Priests of Dachau." *America.* 14 November 1987.

Perszyk, Ken, ed. *Molinism: The Contemporary Debate.* New York: Oxford University Press, 2011.

Plantinga, Alvin. *God and Other Minds: A Study of the Rational Justification of Belief in God.* Ithica, NY: Cornell University Press, 1967.

———, *God, Freedom, and Evil.* New York: Harper Torchbooks, 1974.

———, *The Nature of Necessity.* Oxford: Clarendon, 1974.

Reasonable Faith Forums. "The Greatest Scientific Problem for Christianity." http://www.reasonablefaith.org/forums/choose-your-own-topic/the-greatest-scientific-problem-christianity-6032144.0.html.

Reasonable Faith with William Lane Craig. http://www.reasonablefaith.org.

Rydelnik, Michael. *The Messianic Hope: Is the Hebrew Bible Really Messianic?* Nashville, TN: B&H, 2010.

Satinover, Jeffrey. *Homosexuality and the Politics of Truth.* Grand Rapids, MI: Baker, 1996.

Schmidt, Alvin J. *How Christianity Changed the World.* Grand Rapids, MI: Zondervan, 2001.

BIBLIOGRAPHY

Schneider, John. "Recent Genetic Science and Christian Theology on Human Origins: An 'Aesthetic Supralapsarianism.' " *Perspectives on Science and Christian Faith* 62, no. 3 (September 2010) 196–212.

Scroggs, Robin. *The New Testament and Homosexuality: Contextual Background for Contemporary Debate*. Philadelphia: Fortress, 1983.

Speer, Albert. *Inside the Third Reich*. Translated by Richard Winston and Clara Winston. New York: Simon & Schuster, 1970.

Stackhouse, John. "Just Who Are These 'People of Faith' Anyway." *Christianity Today*, 29 March 2017. Accessed only on electronic edition: www.christianitytoday.com/ct/2017/march/just-who-are-these-people-of-faith-anyway.html (accessed August 2017).

Stark, Rodney. *The Rise of Christianity: How the Obscure, Marginal Jesus Movement Became the Dominant Religious Force in the Western World in a Few Centuries*. San Francisco: HarperSanFrancisco, 1997.

Stenger, Victor. Panel discussion. "Origins and The Big Questions." Skeptics Society Conference. Pasadena, CA: California Institute of Technology, 4 October 2008.

———. Boulder, CO: University of Colorado. Lecture, n.d.

Strobel, Lee. *The Case for a Creator: A Journalist Investigates Scientific Evidence that Points Toward God*. Grand Rapids, MI: Zondervan: 2004.

———. *The Case for Christ: A Journalist's Personal Investigation of the Evidence for Jesus*. Grand Rapids, MI: Zondervan: 1998.

———. *The Case for Faith: A Journalist Investigates the Toughest Objections to Christianity*. Grand Rapids, MI: Zondervan: 2000.

———. *The Case for Grace: A Journalist Explores the Evidence of Transformed Lives*. Grand Rapids, MI: Zondervan: 2015.

———. *The Case for the Real Jesus: A Journalist Investigates Current Attacks on the Identity of Christ*. Grand Rapids, MI: Zondervan: 2007.

———. Highlands Ranch, CO: Cherry Hills Community Church. From a talk given 12 March 2011. Printed by permission.

ten Boom, Corrie. *Father ten Boom: God's Man*. Old Tappan, N.J.: Fleming Revel, 1973.

ten Boom, Corrie, with John Sherrill, and Elizabeth Sherrill. *The Hiding Place*. Old Tappan, NJ: Fleming Revell, 1971.

Vela, Tyler. " 'Slavery' In the Bible—Part 2: Casuistic Laws in the Old Testament." http://freedthinkerpodcast.blogspot.com/2013/06/slavery-in-bible-part-2-casuistic-laws.html (accessed July 2017).

Walton, John, Victor Matthews, and Mark Chavalas. *The IVP Bible Background Commentary: Old Testament*. Downer's Grove, IL: Inter Varsity, 2000.

Weber, Max. *Sociology of Religion*. Boston: Beacon, 1957.

Weikart, Richard. *Hitler's Religion: The Twisted Beliefs That Drove the Third Reich*. Washington, DC: Regnery History, 2016.

Weinberg, Steven. Address, the Conference on Cosmic Design, American Association for the Advancement of Science, Washington, D.C., April 1999.

Williams, Stephen. "The Question of Hell and Salvation: Is there a Fourth View?" *Tyndale Bulletin* 57, no. 2 (2006) 263–83. http://www.tyndale.cam.ac.uk/tb-dates (accessed September 2017).

Wright, David. "Homosexuals or Prostitutes? The Meaning of Arsenokoitai (1 Cor. 6:9, 1 Tim. 1:10)." *Vigiliae Christianae* 38 (1984) 125–53.

www.ingramcontent.com/pod-product-compliance
Lightning Source LLC
Chambersburg PA
CBHW060820190426
43197CB00038B/2170